Remixing the Church

Remixing the Church

The five moves of emerging ecclesiology

Doug Gay

scm press

© Doug Gay 2011

Published in 2011 by SCM Press
Editorial office
13–17 Long Lane,
London, EC1A 9PN, UK

SCM Press is an imprint of Hymns Ancient & Modern Ltd
(a registered charity)
13A Hellesdon Park Road
Norwich NR6 5DR, UK

www.scm-canterburypress.co.uk

British Library Cataloguing in Publication data

A catalogue record for this book is available
from the British Library

978-0-334-04396-6

Originated by The Manila Typesetting Company
Printed and bound by
CPI Antony Rowe, Chippenham, Wiltshire

Contents

For three men who nurtured me in faith:

David Geddes,
Harry Smart,
Lance Stone.

Preface

This book has taken longer than I planned to 'emerge'. I want to thank Bob Hosack of Baker Academic Press for his early encouragement to write it and Natalie Watson of SCM Press for her willingness to publish it and her good and patient advice along the way. Julie Clague, Heather Walton, Lance Stone and Jonny Baker all read the manuscript in draft and gave valuable comments. The book owes much to my times in the alt/emerging communities of the Late, Late Service and Host as well as to conversations with my fellow grandfathers of alternative worship, Jonny Baker and Paul Roberts. Thanks are also due to John Witvliet and Ron Rienstra in Grand Rapids and Irma Fast-Dueck in Winnipeg for generous invitations to present some of these ideas to thoughtful and reflective audiences at the Calvin College Worship Symposium and the Canadian Mennonite University's Refreshing Winds conference. A period of study leave from the University of Glasgow helped provide essential space to write. I want to also thank my wife, Rachel Morley, who has been a creative collaborator and a wise reflector through this journey.

Introduction

Over the last three years, in the time between conceiving this book and writing it, I have become increasingly disillusioned with the debates around the term 'Emerging Church', with both their content and temper. In recent years, the term has been very widely and even promiscuously used by its promoters and has been a constantly moving target for its detractors. This easy mobility has allowed critics to perform highly political operations, which have focused on the aspects that most disturb them and used their analysis of these to discredit (almost) all things associated with it and to warn off the faithful from further exploration.[1]

It may be that we are very close to the end of 'emerging' as a useful term for the Church, and if so, I confess at the outset that I am relaxed about this. I am bored enough with much of both the promotion and criticism to simply let it go and move on. However, I am not yet finally convinced that the term has lost all value for the Church, and at the least I believe it deserves a decent epilogue which offers some sympathetic theological reflection on what all the fuss has been about. This book is my attempt to make a contribution to such an epilogue. It may also be that as the noise level dies down around it, the 'emerging' conversation will maintain and extend its value for at least some of us for a few more years. I have not abandoned that possibility, although it depends on the quality

---

1 I have in mind here, among others, Donald Carson's disappointing treatment *Becoming Conversant with the Emerging Church*, Grand Rapids: Zondervan, 2005, which I feel lacks breadth, nuance and awareness of its topic.

and fruitfulness of the conversation that can be created and sustained.

While I am as vulnerable as the next commentator to betraying my irritation with those who appear to me to be unfair or wrong-headed in their analysis, I mean this contribution to the debate to be irenic and to be modest in the claims it makes. In the midst of academic, online and publishing environments that can take on a shrill and competitive tone, I am convinced that we need to recover and promote a more collegial spirit in which we remain open to correction and revision by other voices. Among other things, the Christian Church is an ongoing conversation with God and with one another about how to live for, with and in God in our own places and times. The temper and character of this conversation is a part of the Church's witness to the gospel and it should always aspire to realize its churchly catholicity – in Miroslav Volf's terms, its inter-ecclesial 'openness'[2] – within its practices of reflection. We are always learning to be the Church, a learning that needs to take place with 'bold humility'.[3] Our calling is therefore not to be theological virtuosi nor to pronounce the last word on our topics, but to play our part in the conversation boldly, while remaining open to correction by sisters and brothers on all sides.

This book is written from within 'the academy', in particular from within the Scottish university where I work as a lecturer in Practical Theology. However, as well as taking 'the Church' for its subject, it also has a more determinative location within the Church and a more determinative vocation to serve the Church. My own working definition of my discipline is that: Practical Theology is the Christian theological practice of reflecting from within the Church on practice in the world,

---

2 Miroslav Volf, *After Our Likeness*, Grand Rapids, MI: Eerdmans, 1998, pp. 156ff. I believe Volf's book represents a significant milestone for ecumenical ecclesiology and his criteria for recognizing 'ecclesiality' are key resources for the emerging conversation.

3 This nice phrase is taken from the title of a 1996 *festschrift* for David Bosch, *Mission in Bold Humility*, edited by W. Saayman and K. Kitzinger, Maryknoll, NY: Orbis, 1996.

including the Church's practice, for the sake of the Church's practice within the mission of God.[4] A shorthand for this would be that it is theology conceived as *Church Pragmatics*.[5]

In my case, the connection to the Church catholic and ecumenical is mediated through the Church of Scotland, a Presbyterian church in the Reformed tradition, and it is in, with and under this connection that I seek to make a contribution here to these international, ecumenical debates about the Church's future. Academic practical theology characteristically tries to maintain the difficult balance of speaking inclusively to both academy and Church and ensuring that its work can be critically assessed and tested by both of these 'publics'. I have tried to do this here, recognizing that some church readers may find parts of the book too 'academic' and some academics may wish for greater rigour.

This book, then, is a provisional attempt to theorize the concept of 'Emerging Church'. I prefer to speak of 'the Church: Emerging', as a conscious attempt to re-weight the term towards ecclesiology – the Christian practice of reflecting on the nature and practice of the Church. I have begun to feel about the phrase 'Emerging Church' the way Stanley Hauerwas talks of his feelings about 'narrative theology' – that the qualifier is in danger of eclipsing the main term.[6] Reversing the order is an attempt to get our theological priorities right, while retaining the qualifier is a claim that the 'emerging conversation' is a potentially fruitful example of 'hermeneutical ecclesiology'.[7] This

---

4   Cf. M. E. Moore, 'Editorial', *International Journal of Practical Theology*, 10:2 (2006), pp. 163–7.

5   With apologies to Karl Barth, this must therefore be *CP* I.1! For more on this vision of theology see my 2006 doctoral thesis available online at: www.era.lib.ed.ac.uk/handle/1842/1699.

6   Stanley Hauerwas, *Performing the Faith*, Grand Rapids, MI: Baker Academic/Brazos, 2004.

7   See Geoffrey Wainwright's impressively concentrated statement: 'The earthly Church is to be understood as an ongoing body in time and space, functioning as a transmissive vehicle and hermeneutical continuum for the original Gospel amid the historically and geographically changing cultures of humankind' (*Worship With One Accord: Where Liturgy and Ecumenism Embrace*, New York: Oxford University Press, 1997, p. 269).

is about how we learn to be Church. Speaking from within the reformed tradition, I am persuaded that there is real continuity and connection between that tradition's idea of 'the Church reforming' and the view of 'the Church: Emerging', which I will be advocating here. I will also argue that there is important common ground between the emerging sensibility[8] and the (modern) ecumenical sensibility.

If we understand ecclesiology as the Church's practice of critical theological reflection upon its own practice, then each of these terms – reformed, ecumenical, emerging – can be seen as (contested) attempts to name a fruitful period of ecclesiological development, in which we learn more about how to be the Church. As such, they take their place beneath primary ecclesiological terms such as the fourfold confession of the Church as one, holy, catholic and apostolic. They represent secondary insights into how to understand and perform that confession faithfully; or, put differently, they are moments within Church *tradition*, in which tradition is a continuing 'godly argument' about how to live as the Church after the likeness of the triune God.[9]

In what follows, I set out a hermeneutical spiral that contains five phases of reflection. I argue that before we bury emergence we might be able to 'parse' it. I suggest that we can explode the term into five moves, which I name as *auditing, retrieval, unbundling, supplementing* and *remixing*. This is, of course, only a heuristic device for mapping the concept of emergence and I am not presenting it as a programme that should or must be followed. In my own case, it represents an attempt to reflect

---

8 For the concept of 'emerging church' as more a sensibility than a movement, see James K. A. Smith, 'Emerging Church: A Guide for the Perplexed', *Reformed Worship*, 77 (2005).

9 I have spoken here about three terms, but a fuller list of analogous secondary terms would include Roman, Eastern/Greek/Russian Orthodox, Calvinist, Lutheran, Anglican, Anabaptist/Baptist, evangelical, Pentecostal, charismatic. For the concept of a 'living tradition' as an extended argument about 'the goods that constitute that tradition', see Alasdair MacIntyre, *After Virtue*, London: Duckworth, 1987, p. 222.

on my own practice within alternative worship[10]/emerging congregations in Scotland and England and on my own participation over two decades in broader national and international networks of debate and discussion.

I suspect that some friends in the alternative worship and emerging networks have at times felt me to be overly conservative, with a rather stubborn continuing attachment to my Reformed and Presbyterian identity and my evangelical roots. If I have at times been a dragging anchor on the journey, I apologize to them for ways in which that has slowed progress in the right direction. The truth is that I, like so many others these days, represent a complex mix of ecclesial influences, all of which have marked me and few of which I wish to disavow entirely. I grew up within the Exclusive Brethren, a paedobaptist sect within the broader Plymouth Brethren movement, and moved over to the Church of Scotland at the age of 16. From my teenage years I was decisively shaped by the evangelical tradition, negotiating my identity in relation to both its Scottish Calvinist and UK/US charismatic streams. Towards the end of my student years I was influenced by a more politicized 'radical' evangelical strand, in particular the work of Scotland's Jim Punton and from North America the work of Ron Sider and of Jim Wallis and the Sojourners Community. It was also at this time that I first encountered the work of the Taizé and Iona communities. I subsequently spent a decade living and working in the multicultural inner city area of Hackney in East London, during which I worshipped and ministered in Reformed churches whose congregations were an exhilarating mix of worshippers from white European and black African, black African-Caribbean and British Asian backgrounds. In the 1990s, as a minister in training with the Church of Scotland, I was involved in establishing an early alternative worship

---

10 For an introduction to these terms reflecting both UK and North American perspectives, see the introductory essay in Jonny Baker and Doug Gay with Jenny Brown, *Alternative Worship*, London: SPCK/Grand Rapids, MI: Baker, 2004; and Ryan Gibbs and Eddie Bolger, *Emerging Churches*, Grand Rapids, MI: Baker Academic, 2006.

congregation, the Glasgow-based Late Late Service. A few years later I was involved in establishing and leading an alternative congregation in London, the Hackney-based HOST congregation.[11] Through all of this, I have participated regularly for over 20 years in the Greenbelt Christian arts festival, which continues to be a crucial UK centre and network for the interchange of ideas and practices related to alternative worship and emerging church.

I mention these stages on my own journey not because I overestimate how interesting I am as an individual, but because they are all, in different ways, intimately connected to the argument of this book. They are markers for the journey I will try to map and the practice on which I seek to reflect.[12]

The concerns of this study are also shaped by my current 'home' within the Reformed tradition. I make no apology for that. The days are gone when academics aspired to the narrative voice of the 'disembodied universal' and today more of us aspire to an honest and reflexive 'standpoint epistemology' recognizing that 'where we sit affects what we see'. Working as I do within an ancient Scottish university, whose Christian DNA has today evolved into fiercely secular shapes, I am constantly urging our ecumenical body of students to *speak from* their own traditions and *listen into* the traditions of others – hoping that we can train ourselves to hear in the accents of particularity not a word of exclusion, but an opportunity for dialogue.

Anticipating the comments of some readers, I am aware that the Church's life is more than its worship and I acknowledge that what follows may at times seem to be overly concerned with that dimension of Church practice. My justification is that this reflects the route by which I have come to the conversations

---

11   Later renamed and repositioned as FEAST (Hackney).

12   In the past several years, I have presented versions of the material in this book at Calvin College in Grand Rapids, at the American Academy of Religion Annual Meeting in Chicago, at the Canadian Mennonite University in Winnipeg and to Church of Scotland groups working on this and related topics. I am grateful to friends (and strangers) in these settings who have given me a hearing and offered helpful feedback and criticism.

about 'emergence' and I fully accept the need for this emphasis to be supplemented by other voices.[13]

In what may also be something of a defence for this book's biases towards worship and mission, it is worth noting that the modern ecumenical movement is incubated in crucial ways within the Liturgical Movement and the 'missionary movement'[14] before it gains its own distinctive articulation in the twentieth century. Here we have at least a precedent for the thought that movements that begin with the remixing of worship ancient and modern or with ventures in cross-cultural mission can be significant for the development of ecclesiology.

I hope that this is both a good-tempered book and one with a sense of its own limitations. It is presented as work in progress – notes and queries offered into a much larger ecumenical conversation – and it looks forward to being corrected and critiqued within that conversation. As such, it emerges itself from a sense of gratitude for the roads taken and in hope for the future of the one, holy, catholic and apostolic Church of which, by God's mercy and grace, we are counted members.

---

13   Geoffrey Wainwright suggests that: 'By virtue of its own symbolic character, the ritual of worship often serves as a focus for matters that occur more widely in doctrine or life' (*Worship with One Accord*, p. 261).

14   On the relationship between the history of missions and the modern ecumenical movement, see among others, David Bosch, *Transforming Mission*, Maryknoll, NY: Orbis, 1990; Timothy Yates, *Christian Mission in the Twentieth Century*, Cambridge: Cambridge University Press, 1996; Andrew Walls and Cathy Ross, (eds), *Mission in the 21st Century*, London: Darton, Longman and Todd, 2008.

'When Were You Robbed?'

Auditing

'Something's missing from my life . . .'
Evan Dando – The Lemonheads

The hermeneutical ecclesiology described here begins with a move I have called 'auditing', a term that today carries a rather 'dry' association with accountancy but, as Walter Ong reminds us in his classic study of orality, has its origins in the practice of checking by 'hearing'.[1] I love the story told by Belfast-based Presbyterian minister and writer Steve Stockman about a cross-community project in which Protestant and Roman Catholic young people visited one another's places of worship as part of a reconciliation programme of encounter and exchange. The visit to the Roman Catholic chapel having duly taken place, the young people headed off to the Presbyterian church. As they all filed in, one young Catholic boy looked around in surprise and said: 'When were you robbed?'

In my case and that of most of the other practitioners and leaders I know of within alternative worship and emerging church settings,[2] the first stage of emergence was marked by a move I will call 'auditing' – a reflexive moment reached within our own development as low church Protestants.[3] As in the Belfast story, this was provoked by experiences and encounters

---

1 Walter Ong, *Orality and Literacy*, London: Routledge, 1982, p. 119.

2 See Appendix A, 'Leaders in Their Own Words', in E. Gibbs, and R. Bolger, *Emerging Churches*, London: SPCK/Grand Rapids, MI: Baker Academic, 2006, where the biographical testimonies largely bear this out.

3 My working assumption is that 'Emerging Church' is a mutation whose origins are decisively located within low church Protestantism.

that challenged us to look and listen beyond the limits and boundaries of our own traditions. In the terms made famous by the Scots philosopher Alasdair MacIntyre, the irruption of such a moment can be read as a vital sign, a sign of life within our experience of church:

> A living tradition then is an historically extended, socially embodied argument and an argument precisely in part about the goods which constitute that tradition.[4]

MacIntyre's notion of an extended argument about constitutive goods can be read as a gloss on 'the grammar of reform' as expressed within the Reformed slogan *Ecclesia reformata, semper reformanda* – 'the Church reformed and always to be reformed'. Reflecting on this 'misused motto', Anna Case-Winters writes that:

> One of the particular gifts of our Reformed tradition is the notion of 'total depravity.' It is one of our least understood gifts to the ecumenical community, but all it means is that we recognize that there is no aspect of our lives that is unaffected by our estrangement from God. Even our best endeavors and highest aspirations are prone to sin and error. Forms of faith and life in the church are no exception. This is why Reformed confessions tend to have their own built-in disclaimers. The preface to the *Scots Confession* invites all readers to offer correction from Scripture if they find the confession to be in error. *The Westminster Confession of Faith* asserts, 'Councils may err and many have erred.'[5]

A reconnection to contemporary critical theory might come by way of the thought that Derridean deconstruction can be fruitfully read as a riff on the Calvinist account of 'total depravity'. James K. A. Smith makes this kind of move in his thoughtful

---

4 Alasdair MacIntyre, *After Virtue*, Duckworth, London, 1987, p. 222.
5 See www.pcusa.org/today/believe/past/may04/reformed.htm.

and provocative book *Who's Afraid of Postmodernism?*, where he takes his readers on 'a tour' of a 'deconstructive church.'[6] Smith's deconstructive *ecclesia* is a community that, he suggests, understands its own postlapsarian (post-fall) condition in terms of a deep 'directional' pluralism,[7] which demands that it engages in a continuous audit of interpretations of scripture and tradition. It is 'called out' of a static, idolatrous and imperialistic understanding of its own identity into a confessional gathering, which tests its own interpretations of the world within the practices of Christian worship and discipleship.

Another way of approaching 'audit' as a theological imperative can be found in Karl Barth's reflections on 'The Holy Spirit and the Gathering of the Christian Community' in *Church Dogmatics* IV.1. Here Barth insists that:

> The *credo ecclesiam* can and necessarily will involve much distinguishing and questioning, much concern and shame. It can and necessarily will be a very critical *credo*.[8]

Barth offers a suggestive distinction between a two-dimensional and a three-dimensional ecclesiology.[9] The 3D Church is the concrete historical church seen not only in (2D) socio-historical terms, nor in (0D/§D?) 'abstract invisibility', but in the 'special visibility' through which its mystery and spiritual character are seen in relation to the power of Jesus Christ and the mission and work of the Holy Spirit.[10] This election of the Church is also for Barth the double-edged sword of its rejection, which means that it can never be anything other than an *église du désert* (a wilderness/tabernacle church).[11] In the face of this continuing

---

6 James K. A. Smith, *Who's Afraid of Postmodernism?*, Grand Rapids, MI: Baker Academic, 2006, p. 57.

7 Smith, *Postmodernism*, pp. 50–1.

8 Karl Barth, *Church Dogmatics* I.1, 'The Doctrine of Reconciliation', Edinburgh: T & T Clark, p. 654.

9 Barth, *Church Dogmatics* I.1, pp. 655ff.

10 Barth, *Church Dogmatics* I.1, p. 656.

11 Barth, *Church Dogmatics* I.1, p. 660.

divine threat Barth rejects any institutional attempt to guarantee the faithfulness (far less the sinlessness) of the Church. Its invisible dimension urges it to, and frees it for, *reform* of its visible life:

> According to its best knowledge and conscience, it can and should create the forms which are indispensable to it as the human society which it essentially is, the forms which are best adapted to its edification and the discharge of its mission . . . But with this reservation in relation to itself, with a consciousness of the relativity of its decisions, their provisional nature, their need of constant reform, standing under and not over the Word . . .[12]

In a searing extended meditation on 'The Being of the Church', as he wrestles with the wound of disunity and the historical separateness of confessional groupings, Barth insists that as believers attend to the real presence of Christ among them, this present Christ will 'dash out of their hands' their 'claim to be identical with the one Church in contrast to others'.[13] Switching metaphors to Paul's imagery in 1 Corinthians 3.12f., he reflects on the proving and trying of our works by fire, from which 'no church will emerge unscathed'.[14]

Here, in an extraordinarily powerful and urgent passage of ecumenical ecclesiology, Barth presses upon us an image of the inescapable ecumenical auditing of our church traditions, as something that is forced upon us by the living presence of Jesus Christ where we are gathered 'two or three' in our separate confessional spaces. There is, then, a double audit involved:

> In the realization of faith in the one Church in face of its disunity, the decisive step is that the divided Churches should honestly and seriously try to hear and perhaps hear the voice

---

12 Barth, *Church Dogmatics* I.1, p. 660.
13 Barth, *Church Dogmatics* I.1, p. 684.
14 Barth, *Church Dogmatics* I.1, p. 684.

of the Lord by them and for them and then, try to hear and perhaps actually hear, the voice of the others. Where a Church does this, in its own place and without leaving it, it is on the way to the one Church.[15]

This final qualification about 'staying in place' is directed against those who would try to flee from the divisions and dis-illusionments of their own confessions into a 'virtual', invisible meta-church. This has much in common with the ahistorical tendency identified by James K. A. Smith as 'primitivism' – the idea of escape from church tradition into a repristinated 'New Testament Church'.[16] At their most idealistic and na-ive, this may be attractive to some 'emerging' groups, but ultimately it is at odds with the grammar of emergence being developed here, because it effectively puts itself beyond 'audit' (and certainly beyond ecumenical audit) into a condition of already realized eschatological alignment with the divine will. It does, however, reflect an impulse not uncommon within the evangelical and charismatic traditions, which have spawned 'emergers', and may be a tendency that will resurface.

Emerging from?

Genealogies of new movements within the Church are often highly contestable, and I have no strong vested interest in try-ing to claim who got where first or exactly who begat whom. Nor do I think that there is a clear research method that could establish exact parameters for mapping the phenomena we are dealing with. I am happy to accept that what came to be called

---

15 Barth, *Church Dogmatics* I.1, p. 684; see also Miroslav Volf, *After Our Likeness*, Grand Rapids, MI: Eerdmans, 1998, p. 156: 'I suggest taking the *openness* of every church toward all other churches as an indispensable condition of ecclesiality' – or as Scots theologian Duncan Forrester was fond of reminding his students, 'Without *them* ye shall not be made perfect'!
16 Smith, *Postmodernism*, p. 129.

'Alternative Worship' in the UK from 1989[17] and 'Emerging Church' in the USA from 1999[18] was in many respects heavily precedented by more isolated and marginal experiments in practice within a range of traditions from at least the 1960s onwards. At present, Gibbs and Bolger's valuable study of *Emerging Churches*[19] remains the most comprehensive account of the origins and development of these two trajectories.[20]

My concern here is not to offer a competing or complementary map or genealogy of the Emerging Church as a movement, but to attempt a reflective 'reading' of the Emerging Church *project* based on a degree of inside experience: a reading which I accept will at times be impressionistic. I will also come clean and accept that I am not pretending only to discover or uncover what is out there, but I am offering a provisional theological articulation of 'emergence', which is bidding to contribute to a definition of it as a project within the Church's life. I say contribute, because the conversation about emergence has exploded exponentially since 1999, particularly in the USA. The huge popularity of the term (not least with publishers!) has produced the double effect that it is both harder to ignore and harder to define. One option, increasingly favoured by some disenchanted insiders, is to accept that the term has simply become a marketing tool and move on. I have some sympathy with this, but I am still convinced that the term may be useful for the Church, particularly if we can generate a degree of consensus about how it might function programmatically. If this attempt fails, it will not be the end of the world – as we noted in the Introduction, the qualifier is not more important than the main term. The key thing is that we have fruitful conversations within the Church about how to be the Church faithfully

---

17 Jonny Baker and Doug Gay, *Alternative Worship*, London: SPCK/ Grand Rapids, MI: Baker, 2004, pp. 19ff.

18 Gibbs and Bolger, *Emerging Churches*, p. 30.

19 Gibbs and Bolger, *Emerging Churches*.

20 See also Paul Roberts, *Alternative Worship in the Church of England*, Grove Booklets, Nottingham: Grove, 1999, for valuable background material.

within contemporary culture. This will be helped by a reduced level of 'hype' and an increased attention to promoting a dialogue which is attentive to a broad range of voices. With those qualifications, I want to explore the kind of 'auditing' that I am suggesting as the initial move within the alt worship/emerging project as it has developed since the 1980s. James K. A. Smith, in his brief 2005 article 'Emerging Church: A Guide for the Perplexed', has suggested that we think about 'emergence' as a broad 'sensibility'. How did this sensibility arise?

Origins

Within the UK, the term 'alternative worship' was coined in the early 1990s as a descriptor for a number of innovative new 'services' inspired by the pioneering and innovative work of a group called the Nine O'Clock Service (NOS), based in the city of Sheffield in the north of England.[21] NOS was based in an evangelical Anglican congregation, which had been strongly influenced by the Charismatic Renewal and, at that point, by the ministry of the late John Wimber.

NOS evolved a new 'hybrid' style of worship, which drew together an unexpected mix of traditions, forms and media. Their services combined elements of Anglo-Catholic and Eastern Orthodox liturgical traditions with influences from charismatic-evangelical spirituality, and set these within a musical-visual medium of communal celebration, which drew heavily on electronic dance/house music and the dance forms of (then) contemporary club culture. The most innovative and unusual feature was that the services used projected visuals, stills and video to create a striking visual environment in the round within which the liturgical action took place. As Jonny Baker and I wrote in the introductory essay to *Alternative Worship*:

---

21 On the history of NOS see, among others, Roland Howard, *The Rise and Fall of the Nine O'Clock Service: A Cult Within the Church?*, London: Mowbray, 1996.

Despite widespread discussion of the significance of living in the age of television, which had been going on within the church since the 1950s, until the Nine O'Clock Service in the late '80s, very few people had made any significant links to a new electronic visual culture in their worship practice. When alternative worship arrived bearing computer graphics, video and slide projection, the churches had literally never seen anything like it. Overnight, worship practice had been launched into late twentieth-century visual culture.[22]

While those who have never experienced this format or have experienced lame examples of it may groan even at the outline description, in aesthetic terms NOS remains among the most striking examples of this I have ever witnessed. There was an artistic boldness and edginess to NOS worship that was both challenging and exhilarating. Walking into the Nine O'Clock Service was like entering into a hybrid of a charismatic worship service, an Anglo-Catholic worship service, a packed and excited club and a postmodern art installation. One striking feature, which set it apart from 1980s' seeker services, was the theological, artistic and technological nous or intelligence that underpinned the performance of the liturgy and the way in which this worked with the grain of popular forms. It was a strange confluence of elitist and anti-elitist forms, which was surprisingly accessible yet which had been combined on the basis of 'artistic' instincts rather than according to the more calculating 'market research' formulations of a seeker service model.

The ultimately tragic story of the rise and fall of NOS has been explored and debated in many forums and I am not going to pursue it here.[23] But the example of NOS is important within this narrative because it launched a broader movement within the UK, which in various ways took up and explored the possibilities of this new hybrid sensibility within worship practice. For me, as for many others who were influenced by

---

22 Baker and Gay, *Alternative Worship*, p. 21.
23 See Howard, *Nine O'Clock Service*, for one account.

it, the example of NOS provoked and crystallized an 'audit' of our traditions of worship practice. This 'audit' took place against a broader socio-cultural background of debate about the 'postmodern' turn within Western societies.

Post-charismatic

In the UK in the late 1980s and early 1990s, those for whom NOS exemplified a critique of their traditions were overwhelmingly those who had been formed within the evangelical/charismatic traditions. The English writer Pete Ward has explored the evolution of charismatic worship culture within the UK and charted North American influences upon it in two important studies: *Growing Up Evangelical* (1996) and *Selling Worship* (2005).[24] In these studies, Ward points out how central 'the worship song' led by 'the worship band' had become to evangelical/charismatic worship practice,[25] rivalling the place of the Eucharist in Roman/Anglo-Catholic worship and the place of the sermon in Reformed worship:

> For the charismatic worshipper, though many still value the sermon and indeed, the act of communion, encounter with God is located primarily in the singing of songs and in the intimate times of prayer and ministry which are often the climax of a time of worship. This means that as the Mass is for Catholics and the Sermon is for Protestants, so the singing of songs for charismatics.[26]

In *Alternative Worship* we named this aspect of the auditing of tradition as a 'post-charismatic' move and detailed some of

---

24 Pete Ward, *Growing Up Evangelical*, London: SPCK, 1996, esp. Chapters 5 and 6; and *Selling Worship*, Milton Keynes: Paternoster, 2005; see also Ward's important recent study *Participation and Mediation*, London: SCM Press, 2008.

25 Ward, *Selling Worship*, p. 1: 'Charismatic worship has become the default setting in most evangelical churches in Britain.'

26 Ward, *Selling Worship*, p. 199.

the cultural, aesthetic and theological dimensions of this turn. There was a rather strong and swift reaction against much of the repertoire of 'worship songs' in circulation and against the medium of 'the worship band'. This was importantly an internal and reflexive critique from a generation of 20 and 30 somethings who had grown up with this music as the principal soundtrack to and expressive medium for their worship practice; it was not the condemnatory voice of 'traditionalists' from the outside, bemoaning the influence of popular culture. It was a protest about the words that were in our own mouths and the tunes to which we knew all the guitar chords. We had become banal to ourselves and felt complicit with a culture of banality in worship. It was a protest against the sing-along 'concert' model of worship, in which a new breed of 'worship leaders' had become a new 'performing clergy' and we their audience-congregation. It was also a protest against the MOR light country/soft rock style that had mainstreamed 'praise and worship music' and deprived it of any musical or lyrical edge.

This 'audit' had already been enabled for some by the growing influence of the Iona Community's Wild Goose Resource Group and in particular the songs of John Bell and Graham Maule. Their early work was strongly based in (mainly Scottish and Irish) folk traditions and represented a distinctively 'unplugged'/left turn away from the dominant musical forms of popular culture. It was genuinely appreciated by many of those who embraced the alt worship turn. They recognized that its content and concerns offered a therapeutic alternative to most contemporary worship songs, but there were reservations about the musical genres involved and its distance from other musical styles within popular culture.

Post-'reformed'/post-evangelical

If the reaction against 'chorus culture' was one of the first moves of the 'alt worship' audit, the NOS model also framed an audit of the broader reformed 'evangelical' Protestant tradition in which alt/emerging practitioners had been formed. Here the emerging movement has appropriated a broad and multifaceted critique of reformed/low church Protestant worship practice. Some aspects of this critique had long existed in parallel traditions and been developed within the Liturgical and Ecumenical movements, while others had come to prominence with the rise of feminist theology and post-colonial theologies of inculturation and contextualization. The comment of the young Roman Catholic visitor to the Reformed church in Belfast expresses a view that was widely owned by emerging practitioners: the starkness of our church interiors, the minimalist aesthetic and the functional values they reflected were increasingly read by ourselves as signs that we had been 'robbed'. An audit of this tradition therefore implied a longer process of tracking back through our tradition to understand how and why this had happened.

Speaking from within a Calvinist-Presbyterian tradition in the Church of Scotland, I am only too conscious that there are many ill-informed and unjust accusations levelled at this tradition in respect of the legacy of Calvin and Knox for culture and the arts. It is important to reject suggestions that the sixteenth-century reformers were simply 'anti-art' or that they had no aesthetic and to affirm the fact that they embraced a different aesthetic.[27] The poet Donald Davie, in his valuable 1978 study *A Gathered Church*, drew on the work of Henry Van Til to speak of a distinctive Calvinist aesthetic, which emphasized 'simplicity, sobriety and measure'.[28] The degree of purging, stripping back and emptying out which marked reformation

27 On 'reformed aesthetics' see the essay of that name by David Fergusson in Duncan Forrester and Doug Gay (eds), *Worship in Context*, London: SCM Press, 2009; see also Paul Corby Finney (ed.), *Seeing Beyond the Word: Visual Arts and the Calvinist Tradition*, Grand Rapids: Eerdmans, 1999; Nicholas Wolterstorff, *Art in Action: Toward a Christian Aesthetic*, Grand Rapids, MI: Eerdmans, 1980; and John W. de Gruchy, *Christianity, Art and Transformation: Theological Aesthetics in the Struggle for Justice*, Cambridge: Cambridge University Press, 2001.

28 Donald Davie, *A Gathered Church: The Literature of the English Dissenting Interest, 1700–1930*, London: Routledge and Kegan Paul, 1978, p. 119.

aesthetics was in its very ruthlessness a bold artistic move. In the sixteenth century it offered 'the shock of the new',[29] a dramatic challenge to refocus the human senses, not least in its invitation to attend to the Word in the language of everyday. The reformers enacted an extraordinary breaking and remaking of common worship, which was as daring in what it gave as in what it took away. We are not yet done with (and perhaps never will be) thinking and rethinking the aesthetic transitions of the Reformation, and I would argue that it is crucial for the future progress of 'emerging aesthetics' that we do not abandon this ongoing task.[30]

That said, however, a crucial move in the development of the alt/emerging sensibility was the recognition that the character of the Reformation had impoverished as well as enriched the life of our churches. Four centuries later, the radical character of that aesthetic and cultural shift and the rich possibilities it offered seemed to have reduced to something much more limited and mundane. The simple void in which something new could be glimpsed too often seemed merely empty. The sobriety that purged the extravagance of medieval kitsch now appeared dull. The measure that refused an aesthetic of excess was too often simply banal. The new disciplines imposed on bodies, intended to liberate them for fresh opportunities in worship, had come to seem restrictive and limiting.

You must not deny the body

A movement that began with the theological warrant, 'If thine eye offends thee pluck it out', had produced 'a generation'[31]

---

29 See Robert Hughes, *The Shock of the New*, London: Thames and Hudson, 1991.

30 See further on this Nicholas Wolterstoff's discussion in *Art in Action*; Frank Burch Brown, *Inclusive Yet Discerning*, Grand Rapids, MI: Eerdmans, 2009; David Fergusson's chapter on 'Reformed Aesthetics', in Forrester and Gay, *Worship in Context*.

31 Though not the whole of a generation – a disaffected faction perhaps.

that was now 'offended' by the working assumption that we were all mouths and ears and lungs. The problem had become one of ecclesiastical bodies, which said to eyes and noses, feet and hands that they were not needed. There was more than a suspicion that the locus of idolatry had simply been shifted and a growing realization that perhaps it always would. The emerging auditors, in keeping with a postmodern, deconstructive spirit, began to explore what was missing, lost, suppressed and repressed within the low church Protestantism in which they had been raised and to ask why.

In my case, as someone formed within the culture of Scottish/UK evangelicalism (and perhaps against many common perceptions), I had continually encountered movements and mentors who were urging me towards a fuller engagement with contemporary culture, politics and the arts. In particular, the influences of the L'Abri movement and of the evangelical student movement UCCF were explicit in their calls for a broad, intellectual engagement in these issues, while Christian festivals such as Scotland's Street Level[32] or the UK-wide Greenbelt[33] were creating spaces for both reflection and performance. There is a case to be made, therefore, that there were intellectual and theological currents allied to these low church traditions that were already forming and schooling a new generation of disciples in fresh modes of thinking and introducing us to artists and thinkers whose influence would be unsettling and provocative.

A text that has intrigued me since my high school years is a powerful illustration of this. T. S. Eliot's 1934 work 'Choruses from *The Rock*' offers a manifesto in miniature for Christian participation in the arts, and crucially insists on the worship space as a key location in which this must be displayed. In

---

32 Street Level was a small Dundee-based festival active in the late 1970s and early 1980s; directed by Andy Thornton and Ricky Ross, among others, it drew in speakers and worship leaders including John Bell and Jim Punton.

33 www.greenbelt.org.uk. Greenbelt was founded in 1974 as a Christian arts festival with a radical evangelical basis.

a passage that asks rhetorically about the range of gifts that should be brought to divine service, Eliot insists that the Creator 'must wish us to create' and use our work of creation in worship:

> For man is joined spirit and body,
> And therefore must serve as spirit and body.
> Visible and invisible, two worlds meet in Man;
> Visible and invisible must meet in His Temple;
> You must not deny the body.[34]

The imperative Eliot had thought within his evolving Anglo-Catholic tradition in the 1930s was given an interesting low church articulation in Ronald Jasper's collection of early essays by members of the Joint Liturgical Group, *The Renewal of Worship*.[35] Here an essay by Baptist liturgical scholar Stephen Winward insists on the theological and biblical case for 'embodied worship'. In the 1970s the new presentations of the body that were appearing within the worship of the Charismatic Movement were accompanied by innovative emphases on the use of dance and visual arts within worship.[36] From another theological angle, the significance of the body was explored in fresh ways within feminist theology in the 1980s,[37]

---

34 T. S. Eliot, 'Choruses from *The Rock*', IX, 1934.

35 Ronald Jasper (ed.), *The Renewal of Worship*, Oxford: Oxford University Press, 1965.

36 For example Patricia Beall and Martha Keys Barker, *Folk Arts in Renewal*, London: Hodder and Stoughton, 1983.

37 On developments in feminist theology in the 1970s and 1980s see, among others, Ann Loades, *Feminist Theology: A Reader*, London: SPCK, 1990; Jenny Daggers: 'Working for Change in the Position of Women in the Church: Christian Women's Information and Resources (CWIRES) and the British "Christian Women's" Movement, 1972–1990', *Feminist Theology*, 26 (2001), pp. 44–69; 'The Rehabilitation of Eve: British "Christian Women's" Theology, 1972–1990', in Susan Frank Parsons (ed.), *Challenging Women's Orthodoxies in the Context of Faith*, Aldershot: Ashgate, 2000, pp. 53–71; 'The Emergence of Feminist Theology from Christian Feminism in Britain', in Charlotte Methuen (ed.), *Time – Utopia – Eschatology*, 1999 Yearbook of the European Society of Women in Theological Research,

leading in the UK to landmark liturgical publications like Janet Morley's *All Desires Known* and the St Hilda Community's *Women Included* book of services and prayers.[38]

If we return to our auditing metaphor (recalling Barth's stress on listening to the voices of others as we reconceive the Church in obedience to the Word) here we begin to see how multifaceted the emerging audit was to become. For the mainstream of low church Protestantism (LCP) and perhaps especially for Reformed streams within that, the voices and practices that were being attended to had long been configured as threatening 'others' whose influence was to be resisted. The 'Catholic/ Anglo-Catholic' traditions had been suspect because of their continuing attachment to 'ritual', read as superstitious and idolatrous by LCP. The charismatic renewal revived and extended elements internal to some traditions of LCP (revivalism, camp meetings, holiness traditions), which had been read since the time of Luther as dangerous 'enthusiasm'.[39] European/Western distaste for these had been given a 'racialized' encoding in the twentieth century with the rise of Pentecostal churches in which white people were criticized for behaving like black people. Finally, the 'other' named by feminist theology was the dangerously sensual 'woman', whose bleeding, birthing, beautiful body had consistently been read by a patriarchal Church as having the potential to both pollute and disrupt public worship.

The emerging audit of reformed and LCP worship was therefore prompted and provoked by a new attentiveness to traditions that had been 'othered' and marginalized over centuries of practice. This attentiveness was forged in diverse and complex ways, as those shaped within LCP traditions increasingly

---

Leuven: Peeters, 1999, pp. 137–44; Susan Frank Parsons, *The Cambridge Companion to Feminist Theology*, Cambridge: Cambridge University Press, 2002.

38 Janet Morley, *All Desires Known*, London: SPCK, 1988; St Hilda Community, *Women Included*, London: SPCK, 1991.

39 Luther's critique of the *Schwärmerei*; revivals were also frequently transgressive of gender roles within worship, as women 'in the Spirit' cried out and prophesied.

encountered these 'others' in the 1980s through a widening circle of reading, ecumenical exchange and, crucially, participation in festivals and conferences.

Three contextual shifts

Three other major contextual shifts also need to be noted here. The first is the broadly diffused influence of the ecumenical movement and of the dissemination in connection with successive World Council of Churches conferences of ecumenical studies on ecclesiology, mission and worship. This was particularly influential on the mainline Reformed churches, despite remaining an object of some suspicion among more evangelical LCP traditions within and beyond the Reformed churches.[40] The second shift is the new climate produced by the Second Vatican Council. It is significant, I think, that the alt/emerging project only emerged in the aftermath of Vatican II: that is, in a climate where the liturgical traditions of the Roman Catholic Church were perceived by a new generation of LCPs as less alien and threatening than they had appeared to their parents. The third major shift was the influence on LCPs of a new wave of missiological thinking, forged in the post-Second World War experience of decolonization. The beginnings of a move towards post-colonial theology produced new ways of thinking about the relationship between theology and culture. The process of debriefing the Western missionary enterprise was gradually producing the therapeutic effect of a new reflexivity within Western churches about their own beliefs and practices and how *they* too were inculturated.[41] Each of these

---

40 See Alister McGrath's fierce critique of the World Council of Churches in his Blackwell manifesto: *The Future of Christianity*, Oxford: Blackwell, 2002, pp. 82ff.

41 The classic study here is David Bosch, *Transforming Mission*, Maryknoll, NY: Orbis, 1991; see also Stephen B. Bevans, *Models of Contextual Theology*, Maryknoll, NY: Orbis, 1992; Lamin Sanneh, *Translating the Message: The Missionary Impact on Culture*, Maryknoll, NY: Orbis, 1989.

shifts produced effects that are still ongoing within the life of many churches in the twenty-first century. For the alt/emerging activists who came from LCP backgrounds, they were crucial factors in creating a new climate of freedom and permission to audit and question church traditions.

We will return to many of these themes in later chapters. Here I have been concerned with trying to establish the basic claim that in conceptual practical theological terms, we can posit a reflexive move of *auditing* as a first stage within a hermeneutical ecclesiology called Emerging Church and with trying to frame a broad description of the particular forms that this move took among LCPs in the UK in the late 1980s and in the UK and North America, Australia and New Zealand in the 1990s.

On a more pastoral note, it is worth noting that auditing is always prone to being a disruptive and divisive process for churches. By its nature, it raises up critical voices and will often draw more attention to what it rejects than to what it affirms. Institutions at their most healthy will ideally maintain a suppleness and an openness to ongoing reform. For many of us, our experience of institutional church is more commonly of a tightly policed conservatism whose resistance to change requires that reformers need to add volume and momentum to their criticism if they are to be heard.[42] In relational terms, this can lead to a recklessness and arrogance on the part of critics who are pained by the resistance to their voices, matched by a stubborn defensiveness on the part of those who are being critiqued, who are wounded by the assault on what they hold dear. Some of the ongoing resistance to 'emerging church' can be traced to the pains inherent in this process, as hard-working and faithful practitioners within a range of churches feel undermined and condemned by criticisms of their way of being Church. There

---

42 In his intriguingly titled volume, *The Emergent Church*, Johann Baptist Metz comments that 'there exists in the church something like a constitutional mistrust of the freedom of the spirit' (London: SCM Press, 1980, p. 108).

is, of course, no easy way through this, but there is a gospel requirement that those provoking and negotiating change seek to be aware of how much 'charity' there is in their words and actions.

In the next chapter, I explore a second hermeneutical move – the practices of *retrieval* within the emerging project.

2

'Searching for Lost Coins'
Retrieval

*Scottish Christians in the later Middle Ages, like their coun-
terparts elsewhere in Britain and on the continent, had a
profoundly sensual experience of religion. The church was
a site of image, sound and smell; the central rite of the mass
celebrated by taste; the whole defined by movement and cer-
emony, and designed to elicit an affective response.*[1]

Postmodern permissions

The move that follows auditing is *retrieval*. If auditing articu-
lated a sense of lack and loss in relation to low church Protestantism, it also stirred a desire to address this. This desire was
awakening within a cultural context, from the 1980s onwards,
which many voices were describing and analysing as postmodern.[2] The term reflects a developing cultural audit of modernity
that was given a number of famous articulations by particular
scholars and thinkers such as Charles Jencks and Jean François
Lyotard, but also had a 'viral' quality. The term caught on;
it stuck with a rising generation because it named a need to
go beyond and *behind* the approach to engaging the world
modernity had constructed for them. The postmodern analysis/
diagnosis carried, among other emphases, the judgement that
'the modern' had both forgotten and suppressed traditions

---

1 M. Todd, *The Culture of Protestantism in Early Modern Scotland*,
New Haven and London: Yale University Press, 2002.

2 For a superb, short introduction to recent debates around postmodernism and how they relate to the Church see James K. A. Smith, *Who's Afraid
of Postmodernism? Taking Derrida, Lyotard and Foucault to Church*,
Grand Rapids, MI: Baker Academic, 2006.

that, for various reasons, had not been seen as useful or fitting. It acted as permission and incentive to go back and explore what had been lost or abandoned along the way.

Staying with my claim that 'emerging church' begins as a reflexive moment within the churches born (directly or indirectly) out of the radical and magisterial reformations, we find that the search for 'lost coins'[3] has been concentrated around the sites associated with these churches' sixteenth-century Reformation revisions of church theology and practice. This is the hermeneutical ecclesiology of the emerging church project understood as what Paul Ricoeur termed a 'hermeneutics of retrieval'.[4]

It will help to ground the argument of this chapter if we look more closely at the kinds of practices and dimensions of the Church's life, which the alt worship/emerging church project has been most interested in retrieving from the neglect or distaste of low church Protestantism. Chief among these are the related concepts of *liturgy* and *ritual*. Within the low church imagination, both liturgy and ritual were seen for centuries as theologically contaminated, as the enemies of grace and as obstacles to the effective working of the Spirit.[5]

Liturgy, in the sense that it was opposed, has been considered problematic for three main reasons. The first had to do with the attempt to 'fix' the content of worship in terms of a specific written script or schedule of items, which specified both content and order. For many low church traditions this approach was inherently wrong, regardless of the 'soundness' or otherwise of

---

3 I am echoing the title of Ann Loades, 1988 study in feminist theology.

4 For an early use of this term see Paul Ricoeur, *Freud and Philosophy: An Essay on Interpretation*, New Haven: Yale University Press, 1970.

5 So Ermanno Genre writes that while Calvin himself 'defended the fundamental function of the rite and ritualism in the service of the gospel . . . (Institutes IV, X, 27, 28) later generations were no longer able to identify with the same degree of clarity *the positive function of rites within the liturgy*' ('Polyphony and Symphony: Protestant Liturgies, a Building Site', in J. F. Puglisi (ed.), *Liturgical Renewal as a Way to Christian Unity*, Collegeville, MN: Pueblo/Liturgical Press, 2005, pp. 133–4).

the content of the liturgy.[6] Appealing above all to the injunction that 'the letter kills, but the Spirit gives life', but frequently invoking also the encouragement to worshippers at Corinth that one should bring a hymn, one a lesson, one a revelation . . . (1 Cor. 14.26ff.), the fixing of worship in script was rejected as contrary to the movement of the Spirit who inspires and animates the Church's worship. The detailed prescription of ritual as to how the bodies of worshippers should be engaged was suspect in part for the same reasons – the fixing of movements or gestures was seen as inherently defiant of the work of the Spirit in directing the body – but a more important LCP anti-ritual discourse has its roots in reformation critiques of ritual as embodying both 'works righteousness' and 'superstition'.

Such resistance was both inspired by and productive of a sensibility that privileged the extempore and the spontaneous – the Spirit sovereignly giving life in real time to the play of voice, posture, movement and gesture within the worshipping community. (At this point we should note that we are faced not just with two competing logics, but two competing aesthetics of the body and its practices in worship.)

A second front for the rejection of liturgy and ritual was the 'Who says?' question about the authorization of liturgy. Here we confront the politics of worship, mediated by patterns of church polity and their various relationships to the state. Most famously, within English language settings, we are familiar with talk of 'the authorized version' as a way of referring to the King James VI/I sponsored translation of the Bible. The rejection of liturgy and ritual on this basis has to do with the rejection of the claim by some political authority – ecclesiastical, monarchical or parliamentary – to 'authorize' the form and content of worship by its moves to permit or prescribe patterns of response and behaviour within worship. The theo-logic at

---

6 On early examples of this hostility see the essay by Bryan D. Spinks on 'The Origins of the Antipathy to Set Liturgical Forms in the English-Speaking Reformed Tradition', in L. Vischer (ed.), *Christian Worship in Reformed Churches Past and Present*, Grand Rapids, MI: Eerdmans, 2003, pp. 66–84.

issue is not (as sometimes suggested) a mere drive for human autonomy, but has to do with the way in which divine sovereignty is operative within the worshipping community. If the authorizing figure or body is denied legitimacy in this sphere, then their attempts to control and legislate what happens in worship must be construed as attempts to pre-empt and resist the sovereign Spirit of God, whose authorization is given more immediately, both internally and communally, to the worshippers themselves as political agents. Once attempts to legislate the content of worship are confronted with this theology of resistance, the non-authorized practices themselves become a mode of dissidence and can be taken as civil and ecclesiastical disobedience. The alternative tradition here comes to be (powerfully) construed in terms of 'dissenting' or 'free' patterns of speech and embodiment.[7]

A third problematic had to do with content. Reformation critiques of Roman Catholic liturgy and ritual were directed at aspects of the prescribed language or behaviour, which were seen to mandate theological mistakes and defy scriptural truths. The 'fixing' of doctrine that takes place within liturgy and ritual has therefore been seen as acting to lock in theological error to the Church's practice.

Taken together these three problematics formed a powerful set of cautions and inhibitions for low church Protestants in respect of liturgy and ritual: attitudes that operated as taboos, as boundary markers, policing the limits of sound practice – marking 'us' off from 'them'. One major effect of this historically was that there was relatively little mixing between major streams of tradition. At the hour of worship, most people were with their own people. In the twentieth century, at conventions, crusades or student fellowships, LCPs were still at home within a broad 'low' church tradition that held divergence over practices such

---

7 By virtue of certain problematic historical anomalies to do with establishment, certain changes to the liturgical uses and practice of the Church of England (though not the Church of Scotland) still require the approval of the UK parliament.

as baptism within a common 'evangelical' or 'reformed' culture. Low church identity here functioned as a kind of invisible denomination, whose habits and rules worked across visible denominational boundaries to bracket the high church possibilities available within some of these denominations.

For the emerging church movement of *retrieval* to take place, two things were therefore necessary. First, there had to be a loosening of the cultural and theological inhibitions, which put other modes of being the worshipping church out of bounds. Second, it was necessary for there to be opportunities for encounter with and experience of other modes of church, but these encounters had to make alternative traditions available for retrieval in ways that were non-threatening. This last point is particularly significant because it stresses the importance to the emerging project of being able to appropriate and retrieve alternatives from a low church starting point, without being subsumed into them. The alternative here would be not retrieval, or *ressourcement*, but wholesale conversion into another 'higher' tradition.[8]

Natural exclusions: forgetting *why* we *didn't do* that

For those unfamiliar with the ways and means of low church Protestantism, there may be a tendency to underestimate the extent to which a project of retrieval remained a transgressive project for those formed within these precincts. Recalling James K. A. Smith's observations about *primitivism*, we are reminded that the very idea of 'tradition' had acquired a certain 'taboo' status, seen in the way that a number of evangelical

---

8 Here, as well as the obvious celebrated examples such as Newton in the nineteenth century, we could compare the more recent moves by commentators such as Mike Riddell, a New Zealand Baptist commentator influential within emerging circles who converted to Roman Catholicism or Professor Andrew (Deep Church) Walker, who converted to Orthodoxy some years ago, from a background in the Charismatic House Church in the UK.

theologians[9] explicitly rejected the notion of a threefold source for Christian theology (scripture, tradition, reason) as opening the door to unscriptural and anti-scriptural innovations. While the target of such critiques was what we might call a 'strong' view of tradition, the effect was to bring other uses of the term under a certain cloud of suspicion and to suggest that church practice could somehow be guided by a recourse to scripture that was uncontaminated by 'tradition'.

The habits of practice meant that the bodies of worshippers within the low churches were accustomed to certain exclusions – that these had become 'natural'. In MacIntyre's terms, these were issues about which the arguments were perceived as 'over and done with' and settled judgements about the goods of the tradition were seen to have already been achieved. Acts of retrieval were therefore liable to be perceived as inherently transgressive, although this always begged the question of precisely what and whose boundaries were being crossed. As their members became accustomed to certain exclusions and these exclusions became wholly 'natural' to them, the precise theo-logics involved had been widely forgotten within the low churches. There was a wide range of things which those like us 'just didn't do', but up to 400 years after many of these exclusions had first been fixed on, their rationale had often been both neglected and forgotten. This accumulated forgetfulness lowered the resistance of low church traditions to acts of trespass and retrieval. What made such acts both more possible and more likely, though, was the coincidence of such a lowering of the Protestant guard with a wider rehabilitation of tradition which had philosophical, theological and ecclesial dimensions.

The philosophical rehabilitation of 'tradition'

The metaphor of retrieval can be linked to a number of intellectual and cultural counter-currents within the development of

---

9 For example, J. I. Packer, *Truth and Power*, Wheaton, IL: Harold Shaw, 1996.

modernity. The broad stirring of sensibilities named as Romanticism, which drew some of its impulse from German Pietism, developed through the later eighteenth century and gained further momentum in the nineteenth century as a counterpoint to the modernizing processes of industrialization and urbanization. The retrieval of what was beautiful, classic and valuable from previous historical eras was one of the key concerns of Romanticism, not just for antiquarian reasons (although 'antiquarianism' also became popular in this era) but for poetic and rhetorical reasons. Across continental Europe, the early work of what was later christened the Liturgical Movement exemplified these themes. In Britain, particularly though not exclusively in England, and most particularly in relation to the Church of England and Roman Catholic Church, there were a number of significant religious and theological articulations of 'romantic retrieval' in relation to religious art (pre-Raphaelite), church architecture (Gothic Revival), church order and church liturgy (Oxford Movement).[10] The mid nineteenth century saw a further elaboration of 'high church' as an ecclesial and liturgical sensibility and 'style' and its increasing fusion with the term 'Anglo-Catholicism'.

The philosophical currents of romanticism flowed on into the twentieth century and a range of anti-modernist movements waxed and waned in various decades, some more benign than others. In some cases, tradition was associated with a 'conservative' stewardship of the inheritance of high culture, in others it was related to an 'organicist' remembering of folkways and mythologies. In philosophical hermeneutics, the theme of 'tradition' was given new prominence in the work of Hans-Georg Gadamer, in particular his 1960 *Truth and Method* in which he argued that typically the act of understanding takes place as a fusion of horizons past and present. Another key

---

10 Key figures here include Augustus Welby Northmore Pugin, John Ruskin, John Henry Newman and Thomas Carlyle. Arguably, the work of John Nelson Darby, a founder of the Plymouth Brethren, can also be read through the lens of Romanticism, although in his case it is 'primitivism' rather than 'catholicism' that is to the fore.

influence on reframing and 'rehabilitating' the idea of tradition in the 1980s was the work of Scottish philosopher Alasdair MacIntyre. In *After Virtue*, MacIntyre emphasized that:

> *all* reasoning takes place within the context of some traditional mode of thought . . . when a tradition is in good order it is always partially constituted by an argument about the goods the pursuit of which gives to that tradition its particular point and purpose.[11]

By the 1990s, the influence of Gadamer and MacIntyre and the developing debates around postmodernism reflected an intellectual climate in which the concept of tradition was opening out towards a more supple and dialogical understanding in which arguments about the goods of Christian practice could be traced and explored across a wide range of historical sources. This climate offered conditions in which the distinctive emphases of 'emerging church' could begin to develop.

A theological rehabilitation of 'tradition'

Talk of theological rehabilitation of tradition may sound alien or unnecessary to some from what I have loosely called 'high church' contexts, but in fact, there are rehab stories to tell across the denominational spectrum. The nineteenth century saw distinct but related theological movements within Roman Catholic, Anglican and Presbyterian churches which emphasized the crucial role played by 'deep' tradition in reforming liturgy and articulating a clear understanding of (catholic) church order. In the early decades of the twentieth century, the beginnings of organized ecumenical encounter created new dialogical settings within which it was important for participants to bring their stories to the table. While ecumenism might by definition seem to suggest a more fluid and relativizing

---

11 A. MacIntyre, *After Virtue*, London: Duckworth, 1987, p. 222.

perspective on tradition, in practice there is also a certain hardening associated with narrating and representing your own tradition to others. Ecumenical theology has therefore exhibited a double tendency with regard to 'tradition', both relativizing and rehabilitating it, as a condition of the possibility of its own discourse.[12]

From the 1930s, the work of Karl Barth and others associated with 'neo-orthodox' theology involved a significant recourse to tradition in opposition to a 'liberal' theological modernism. However, Barth's refusal simply to venerate tradition or ascribe it intrinsic authority is perhaps most clearly seen in his declaring for *credo* as opposed to *paedo* baptism. In this connection, he could maintain that the Church's practice had been 'irregular' for some 1,500 years.[13] Around the same time, Roman Catholic theologians associated with the *nouvelle théologie* were defending their relationship to 'tradition' by means of the metaphor of *ressourcement*, which was to become one of the two guiding metaphors of the Second Vatican Council.

For most low church Protestants, who prized the Reformation cry *ad fontes*, the work done under this banner had been absorbed almost without remainder into their doctrine of scripture. Trevor Hart comments that 'Tradition is one of those "light the blue touch paper and retire to a safe distance" words'.[14] In his endorsement of Daniel Williams' 2005 book *Evangelicals and Tradition*, David Neff makes the pithy

---

12 While I stand by the view that to some degree reflection and dialogue on tradition(s) was intrinsic to early ecumenical gatherings, I note Daniel Williams' suggestion that 'Constructive and interchurch dialogue on the matter of tradition was not taken up until the Faith and Order conferences of the WCC held at Lund in Sweden 1952 and Montreal 1963' (*Evangelicals and Tradition: The Formative Influence of the Early Church*, Grand Rapids, MI: Baker Academic, 2005, p. 20).

13 Barth's later position on baptism is outlined in Volume IV.1 of *Church Dogmatics*; his first signal of dissent from the paedobaptist consensus of the reformed tradition came in *The Teaching of the Church Regarding Baptism*, London: SCM Press, 1948.

14 T. Hart, *Faith Thinking*, London: SPCK, 1995, p. 165.

observation that 'Tradition used to be a "fightin' word" for Protestants'.[15] Williams' own significant contribution from the 1990s was predated by that of US scholar Thomas Howard, in *Evangelical Is Not Enough*,[16] and, most influentially, by the work of US theologian Robert Webber. Webber's project can be dated back to his significantly titled early volume *Common Roots* (1968), but became more influential after his somewhat controversial (he was then teaching at Wheaton College) 1985 publication *Evangelicals on the Canterbury Trail: Why Evangelicals are Attracted to the Liturgical Church*.[17] Webber's work was influenced by and associated with that of Thomas C. Oden, after the latter's 1979 turn to 'paleo-orthodoxy', but Webber's contribution has generally been given a warmer and wider welcome than Oden's.[18] Webber's 'ancient-future' descriptor[19] was cited by Gibbs and Bolger as a key identifier of *Emerging Churches* and his work is widely known and discussed within the emerging conversation. The work of Daniel Williams, already mentioned above, who along with Baker Publishing has coined the term *evangelical ressourcement*,[20] has now moved to the forefront of evangelical debates about the status of tradition. A more rarefied but still significant influence since the early 1990s has been the English-based Radical Orthodoxy movement, which has promoted significant alignments

---

15 Neff's comment is printed on the dust jacket.

16 Nashville: Thomas Nelson, 1984. Howard's 'turn' to Roman Catholicism was given additional poignancy by his being the brother of evangelical icon Elizabeth Elliot. His interest in C. S. Lewis also highlights a common point of engagement between evangelicals and Anglo-Catholicism.

17 Waco, TX: Word Books, 1985.

18 Webber has been a key influence within emerging church conversations, while Oden's work is rarely mentioned.

19 For a summary of Webber's position see his jointly authored 'A Call to an Ancient Evangelical Future', as well as his individual volumes *Ancient-Future Faith* and *Ancient-Future Evangelism*. See also the volume of papers from the 2007 Wheaton Theology Conference: M. Husbands and J. P. Greenman (eds), *Ancient Faith for the Church's Future*, Downers Grove, IL: InterVarsity Press, 2008.

20 Williams' use of this term dates from around the same time as my own independent attempts to link it to discussions around emerging church.

with Roman Catholic *nouvelle théologie* and their agenda of *ressourcement*.[21] In a similar vein, the work of Stanley Hauerwas has been influential in promoting a positive attitude to 'catholic/Catholic' tradition in corners where this was uncommon.[22] The view from 2010, 100 years after the symbolic beginnings of the ecumenical movement, displays a wide range of theological positions on 'tradition', such that it is no longer only the 'fightin' word' for (low church) Protestants that it was once.[23]

Inherited knee-jerk reactions to 'tradition' have been abandoned by those involved in the emerging church conversation, but that lack of deference survives in a continuing willingness to make or defend Barth-like judgements about theological questions where wholesale departure from key aspects of tradition is required. While Barth promoted this type of radical criticism of tradition in relation to baptism, Hauerwas, in his alignment with John Howard Yoder, is making a comparable move in relation to non-violence. Meanwhile, most mainline Protestants (the Anglicans still lag behind a little here) have now moved to embrace a major critical revision of the tradition in respect of the ordination of women.

Even within a more open and diverse theological landscape, therefore, we are not done with the vexing task of negotiating

---

21 For example, Simon Oliver's introduction to the *Radical Orthodoxy Reader*, London, Routledge, 2009, p. 28; John Milbank, who I greatly admire in many respects, has written a pompous and anglo-centric but otherwise unimpressive sneer at emerging church initiatives in the shape of his 'Stale Expressions', *Christian Ethics*, 21:1 (2008), pp. 117–28. Among those associated with the Radical Orthodoxy collective, the work of D. Stephen Long and James K. A. Smith shows most willingness to engage in a productive dialogue with the emerging church conversation.

22 See, among many possible examples, his Gifford Lectures, *With the Grain of the Universe*, Grand Rapids, MI: Brazos/London: SCM Press, 2001.

23 Here we can also compare the recent attempts to promote a 'Deep Church' tradition, led by Andrew Walker and Luke Bretherton (eds), *Remembering Our Future: Explorations in Deep Church*, Milton Keynes: Paternoster, 2007.

the theological status of church tradition. The Reformation watchword of *sola scriptura* has traditionally been understood as establishing a clear hierarchy between scripture and tradition, such that some Protestant theologians have been uncomfortable with using a single term like 'source' to designate both. A defence of that hierarchy may still be seen as legitimate and even necessary, but it must reckon with the tendency of such a theological move to lead to a theoretical deficit in LCP accounts of tradition. In particular, questions of authority within ecclesiology have received very little attention within emerging church conversations.

We will return to this important question in the following chapter, but I raise it here to point to the combination of freedom and reticence with which the emerging project tends to approach church 'tradition'.

The new freedom to 'love' and embrace tradition has been acquired without surrendering the low church Protestant sense that tradition can always be trumped because it is not a 'source' on a par with scripture and because the *magisterium* which has authorized traditional formulations is equally prone to error and self-deception in every age of the Church's life.

As in the wider low church Protestant world, this insistence on relativizing the status of tradition is often accompanied by an underdeveloped theological capacity for evaluating tradition, marked by a lack of vocabulary. If tradition is not a source, what is it and how should it be treated?

From the perspective of practical theology, this theological chestnut may be rescued from a set of sterile oppositions when we approach it by reflecting on what congregations are doing. Theology as 'Church Pragmatics' is unlikely to be comfortable with *lex orandi, lex credendi* or its opposite, just because of its attentiveness to practice (including the practice of *credendi*). At the end of this chapter we will look more closely at the kinds of practices that have been retrieved by 'emerging churches'. Before that, we consider some broader moves within church practice, which have contributed to the rehabilitation of tradition.

The ecclesial rehabilitation of 'tradition'

For many Protestant churches, the seventeenth and eighteenth centuries were marked by a tendency towards liturgical 'deflation' or 'reduction', which consolidated the de-Romanizing moves of the sixteenth century.[24] This liturgical reduction[25] did not in any sense mean that patterns of worship were static and unchanging, but that where notable changes took place, they tended to reflect the various ways in which the 'purified' patterns of worship found new modes of performance and popular inculturation in Western societies. The rise of Pietism, Revivalism, Methodism and Evangelicalism in the eighteenth century was hugely significant for future developments in ecclesiology and liturgy, but these movements often shared a common 'primitivist' tendency in ecclesiology and a sense that spirit-filled worship could thrive and reach new intensities within the reduced liturgical palette of low church Protestantism.[26]

The Liturgical Movement

One of the earliest signs of a new move towards renewing (re-olding?) liturgy by means of a retrieval of ancient texts can be seen in the eighteenth-century appropriations of the Liturgy

---

24 So Howard G. Hageman could suggest that Reformed liturgies 'proliferated in the sixteenth century, died in the seventeenth and were buried in the eighteenth' ('Three Lectures', in Gregg Mast, *In Remembrance and Hope: The Ministry and Vision of Howard G. Hageman*, Grand Rapids, MI: Eerdmans, 1998). In similar terms Elsie Anne McKee emphasized that in the early days of the Calvinist Reformation, 'Protestants generally agreed on the usefulness of having a prepared text for most parts of the service . . . Putting the words of prayer and praise in the mouths of the whole congregation was vital' ('Reformed Worship in the Sixteenth Century', in Lukas Vischer (ed.), *Christian Worship in Reformed Churches Past and Present*, Grand Rapids, MI: Eerdmans, 2003, pp. 9, 19).

25 As in cooking, a reduction can produce increased potency.

26 The reduction was commonly seen as a restoration of primitive liturgical patterns, with the accretions of medieval Catholicism stripped away.

of Saint James of Jerusalem by the non-jurist tradition of the Scottish Episcopal Church.[27] Their efforts were harbingers of a broader nineteenth-century enterprise, which became known as the Liturgical Movement.[28] While I understand the concerns of those who wish to use this term in a narrower sense to describe only a movement within the Roman Catholic Church, I am using it here in its broader sense to refer to an ecumenical constellation of related efforts and effects, reaching back, for example, to the Scottish Episcopal Church's work in the eighteenth century and reaching out to embrace the spectrum of nineteenth- and twentieth-century Protestant interests in liturgical retrieval.

The Liturgical Movement was fuelled by a desire for retrieval of pre-modern liturgical patterns and practices, not just for historical or archival reasons but with the aim of renewing the contemporary worship practice of the Church. Within the Roman tradition, the iconic initiatives of Dom Prosper Guéranger at Solesmes from 1832, of Beauduin's address to the 1909 Mechelen Congrès, along with his work at Louvain and Herwegen and Casel's at Maria Laach, and the founding of the Centre de Pastorale Liturgique in Paris in 1940, contributed to a stream of liturgical revision that would deepen and broaden as it combined with the reflective work of the *nouvelle théologie* and flowed on into the liturgical revisions of Vatican II.[29] Alongside this major channel, however, there were other tributaries and streams within the Protestant world, which made up the broader 'liturgical movement' through their various engagements in a critical and selective retrieval of

---

27 Of this 1764 Liturgy Geoffrey Wainwright writes: 'Here was an attempt at repristination which cut back behind the limitations and distortions of both the Roman and the Protestant West in order to recapture an earlier balance and fullness which the Byzantine and some other Eastern churches had preserved' (*Doxology*, New York: Oxford University Press/ London: Epworth Press, 1980, p. 333).

28 'The modern Liturgical Movement, which began roughly with our century, but whose first full compositions appeared only after the Second World War' (Wainwright, *Doxology*, p. 334).

29 On the *nouvelle théologie* see Fergus Kerr's introduction in David Ford (ed.), *The Modern Theologians*, Oxford: WileyBlackwell, 1996.

worship traditions. While the most famous of these was the nineteenth-century Oxford or 'Tractarian' movement within the Anglican tradition, the Church of Scotland also developed its own distinctive channels of reception and production which drove major changes in worship practice in Victorian Scotland and were influential across international English-speaking Presbyterian and Reformed networks.[30]

Geoffrey Wainwright observes, in relation to the modern Liturgical Movement's return to biblical and patristic sources:

> For the Roman Catholic Church the return has meant a purification. Ritual, ceremonial and calendrical excrescences have been docked in a great process of simplification. Roman unilateralisms have been corrected by being set within a geographically wider patristic context and a more scriptural context of interpretation. The 'new mass' illustrates all this . . . [in contrast] for [Protestants] the rediscovery of patristic structures and themes has contributed not so much a purification as an enrichment.[31]

The Ecumenical Movement

The twentieth century saw the beginnings of organized ecumenism take their most concrete shape in the missionary movement-inspired World Missionary Conference held in Edinburgh in 1910.[32] Of the various continuation groups and processes

---

30 On the Scoto-Catholic movement, see Stewart J. Brown's essay in D. Forrester and D. Gay (eds), *Worship and Liturgy in Context*, London: SCM Press, 2009.

31 Wainwright, *Doxology*, p. 336; the new mass he refers to is the post-Vatican II Missal.

32 'At which the testimony from the "overseas" mission fields concerning the "scandal" of Christian disunity as an obstacle to evangelization started to put pressure on the "home" churches to set their own house in order' (G. Wainwright, *Worship With One Accord: Where Liturgy and Ecumenism Embrace*, New York: Oxford University Press, 1997, p. 259).

that emerged from the 1910 conference, the Faith and Order trajectory was primarily concerned with questions of shared belief and practice, including worship and ecclesiology. This inter-church process, which would later be institutionally in-corporated into the World Council of Churches (WCC) from 1948, benefited from the pre-existing international, interde-nominational flows of the Liturgical Movement, but it also dramatized and exposed the extreme difficulties that the vari-ous churches would experience in achieving mutual recogni-tion and reconciliation in areas where they had historically been divided.

The history of institutional ecumenism in the twentieth and twenty-first centuries has been mostly slow and often painful, with few of the gains in terms of visible unity dreamed of by the pre-1948 pioneers.[33] But the Ecumenical Movement, conceived of as the myriad local, regional and national, bilateral and mul-tilateral processes of dialogue and co-operation between a host of Christian denominations, has been profoundly influential in establishing a more generalized culture of mutual respect. This must also be named as a significant factor in the ecclesial reha-bilitation of tradition, since the conciliar processes of the WCC streams and their informal, localized analogues have involved members of many churches in giving an account of their own history and attending to that of others. Karl Barth's observa-tions, quoted in the previous chapter, reflect his own long ex-perience of ecumenical dialogue, in WCC forums and latterly as a commentator on Vatican II. This may seem like an em-barrassingly modest claim to make for so much accumulated

---

33 Alongside more formal histories of ecumenism, biographies like Keith Clements', treatment of J. H. Oldham in *Faith on the Frontier*, Edinburgh: T & T Clark/Geneva: World Council of Churches, 1999; Willem Visser t'Hooft's *Memoirs*, London: SCM Press, 1973; and Lesslie Newbigin's au-tobiography *Unfinished Agenda*, Edinburgh: St Andrew Press, 1993, offer more readable and illuminating accounts of the same material. For a harsher verdict on the World Council of Churches, see Alistair McGrath's Blackwell manifesto *The Future of Christianity*, London: Blackwell, 2002.

ecumenical effort, but in the context of a study of the Emerging Church, it is a crucial one.

Under this heading and despite its refusal to become a member of the World Council of Churches, we should also note the crucial influence of the sweeping internal reforms within the Roman Catholic Church, following the Second Vatican Council. These reforms, particularly those of the Church's worship, were signalled in *Sacrosanctum Concilium*, the first document to be approved by the Council in 1963.[34] They have been hugely significant in creating a generation of post-Vatican II Protestants, who no longer carry the same suspicions and antipathies towards Roman Catholic identity and practice as that of their parents' generation.[35] The dismantling of barriers to understanding and encounter brought about not least by the introduction of the vernacular mass, has been a crucial factor in creating a new openness among low church Protestants to exploring and retrieving the liturgical inheritance of pre-Reformation traditions.[36]

Accessing *catholic* tradition

These large-scale processes – the Liturgical and Ecumenical movements and the Vatican II reforms – have influenced the contemporary Church in a variety of ways. However, they have been mediated to those involved in the projects of 'emerging church' in particular through the witness of two European communities which have had a growing international influence

---

34 For one account of the outworking of the reforms (in Scotland) see Michael Regan's 'The Reception of the Liturgical Changes of the Second Vatican Council', in Forrester and Gay (eds), *Worship and Liturgy in Context*.

35 As Williams says: 'Protestants of all stripes must comprehend once and for all that "catholic" is not the opposite of "Protestant"' (*Evangelicals and Tradition*, p. 15).

36 For example, and perhaps ironically, Protestants seem to have found singing Latin chants in worship more congenial, once Latin had been abandoned as the prescribed language for Mass.

on worship and spirituality in the period since the Second World War. The Iona Community, founded in 1938, and the Taizé Community, founded in 1949, were both products of the Liturgical and Ecumenical movements. As their influence has grown, primarily through the reception and transmission of their liturgical practices, they have functioned as portals into 'catholic' tradition for millions of low church Protestants across the world.[37] This liturgical experience of encountering 'catholic' tradition has often taken place in boundary or threshold settings, where people gather beyond their local congregations. In the UK the Greenbelt festival has been a key location, where perhaps 100,000 people have experienced something of the worship practice of the Iona Community over the past 25 years. Others have encountered this worship through one of the thousands of local or regional training events and ecumenical conferences led by the Wild Goose Resource Group over a similar period. This contact has been reinforced and extended through cycles of 'consumption' and circulation of the community's published liturgical resources and recordings.[38] The patterns and practices of 'Iona worship' are then taken back home by church and worship leaders, who introduce them to local congregational settings.

A similar pattern can be seen with Taizé worship, where pilgrimages to Taizé offer brief periods of immersion in the community's worship, and large urban Taizé gatherings in cities such as London, Edinburgh and New York (some supported directly by brothers from Taizé) allow wider groups to encounter Taizé patterns and practices. The liturgical circuit is then completed, as with Iona, by music and liturgy being taken back into local congregational settings.

---

37 See 'The Worship of the Iona Community and its Global Impact', by Norman Shanks (a former leader of the Iona Community) in Forrester and Gay (eds), *Worship and Liturgy in Context*. For a recent reflection on the influence of the Taizé Community see Pete Ward, *Participation and Mediation: Practical Theology for the Liquid Church*, London: SCM Press, 2008, pp. 185–6.

38 Ward, *Participation and Mediation*, pp. 185–6.

Clearly, Christians from a wide range of denominational traditions have been influenced by these connections. The particular point being made here is that for worshippers from low church Protestant settings, they have been a crucial means of encounter with 'catholic' liturgical tradition. The status of both Taizé and Iona as ecumenical *communities* and not competing denominations has rendered them less threatening to these worshippers' existing theological and liturgical habits. So church people whose worship practice had been more or less exclusively 'low,' and in particular those from evangelical and charismatic backgrounds, have increasingly found themselves, from the 1980s onwards, using written liturgies with congregational responses, singing – in Greek or Latin as well as English – *Kyries*, *Glorias*, the *Agnus Dei* and *Veni Sancte Spiritus*, and engaging with new forms of intentional ritual that involve lighting candles, kneeling and laying on of hands.

Here again, I want to appeal for the patience of readers who are not familiar with low church tradition. I am aware of how conventional these patterns and practices have been to Roman Catholics, the Orthodox, many Anglicans and even some Methodists and Presbyterians. I understand, too, that the influence of the Liturgical and Ecumenical movements was already well advanced within the mainline Protestant denominations by the 1980s. My concern here is to stress that for many low church traditions – Baptist, Brethren, Congregationalist, Independent Evangelical, Pentecostal denominations and Independent Pentecostal churches, new 'charismatic' churches and networks, as well as many conservative and charismatic evangelical congregations within the Anglican, Methodist and Presbyterian churches – such ways of worshipping remained deeply alien. In a few settings the rationales for proscribing them were perhaps still current, while in many others they were largely forgotten; in either case most worshippers in these churches lacked sympathetic contexts in which to encounter or experience liturgical alternatives. It was not only or exclusively Taizé and Iona which offered points of encounter and access; but over an extended period they were among the most important bridging and mediating influences within the UK. Another influential strand, particularly in the US but also to a degree in the UK, was the interplay of evangelical and Roman Catholic influences in the pages of *Sojourners* magazine from the 1970s. The work of the evangelical Quaker Richard Foster, in particular his widely read book *Celebration of Discipline* (1978), was also another important point of connection with traditions and practices of 'catholic' spirituality in both the UK and North America.

I appeal for patience also from those whose immediate reaction might be to judge that these encounters represent only a shallow or superficial consumer encounter with catholic tradition. For those of us who were born and raised at some remove from these liturgical settings, a journey of discovery and 'reception' has to start somewhere. What may try the patience of some readers more than the fragmentary and partial character of these initial encounters is the way in which I will go on to argue for the necessity of a critical and partial reception of 'catholic' tradition. That argument belongs within the next move of 'unbundling'.

I will return to these questions from a different angle and in some more detail in the next chapter, but here I want to move towards a more concrete account of the kinds of resources and practices that some of those associated with the emerging project have been most interested in retrieving.

Retrievers

In a rather dismissive contribution to a 2008 collection of essays, *Evaluating Fresh Expressions*, English theologian Martyn Percy, noting the interest in liturgical tradition within many 'emerging' congregations, turns the witty phrase 'teaching new dogs old tricks'.[39] (In the context of this book, the dogs in

---

39 In Martyn Percy and Louise Nelstrop (eds), *Evaluating Fresh Expressions*, Norwich: Canterbury Press, 2008; Jonny Baker's well-known and

question must be presumed to be retrievers.) Although it was clearly not intended as a compliment, I have no problem with this as a characterization of one part of the emerging project. In this final section, I want to describe some of the old tricks that the emerging dogs have been learning.

The church year

One good place to start is with time and how it is inhabited and experienced. In contrast to what Charles Taylor calls the empty or flat time of secular society,[40] catholic tradition has long carried an alternative vision of time under God, which is named and divided liturgically. The sixteenth-century reformers, reacting to an over-elaborated and over-engineered late medieval articulation of the Christian year, swept much of it away at a stroke and their successors in the seventeenth and eighteenth centuries allowed what was left to reduce still further. All that was left for most Presbyterians at the beginning of the nineteenth century was a rigorous Sabbatarianism, from which even minimal observance of Christmas and Easter had been purged. Similarly, many raised among Brethren, Baptists, Mennonites or Pentecostals can testify to being told that 'every Sunday was Easter/Christmas' (which also meant, of course, that no Sunday ever was). The Liturgical Movement in its widest ecumenical articulation spread an enthusiasm for retrieval of the liturgical calendar, and in its narrower, Roman Catholic articulation prepared the way for substantial reforms to the Roman version of the calendar at Vatican II. As Geoffrey Wainwright noted in the quotation cited earlier, the reforms of the Second Vatican Council encouraged an ecumenical

---

much-visited website draws on the metaphor of the 'trickster' as discussed by Lewis Hyde in *Trickster Makes This World* (Edinburgh: Canongate, 2008), to identify innovative possibilities in worship as 'worship tricks'; see http://jonnybaker.blogs.com/jonnybaker/.

40 Charles Taylor, *A Secular Age*, Cambridge, MA and Belknap: Harvard University Press, 2005, p. 124.

convergence around a simpler shape with a clearer Christologi-
cal focus (the more elaborate or controversial Roman survivals
have simply been ignored by most Protestants). Those involved
in the alt/emerging project have here gone with the flow of
mainline Protestant denominations in embracing a core liturgical calendar. For some who grew up within such mainstream
contexts this has been unremarkable. For others who were mi-
grating from lower settings their first real exposure to this came
through their encounter with emerging groups.

Set prayers and classic shapes

I try to travel fairly light to theological pedantry, but one of
my biggest exceptions is reserved for use of the word 'liturgical' and in particular to the horrible phrase 'liturgical worship'.
Common usage in church history requires reference to the Liturgical Movement, but I have no truck with talk of 'the liturgy' singular. I stand with those who insist that every worship
gathering has 'a liturgy', is 'liturgical'. As a practical theologian
what interests me is attending to 'the shape of the liturgy being
practised' and to the liturgical choices made within it in any
given place and time.

The rehabilitation of set or written prayers has been an ongoing process within Protestant worship for some two centuries
now. Those not used to this taboo may find it hard to fathom,
but conceding that a ready-made, written-down prayer could in
principle be fit for use in worship has been and continues to be a
major shift for many low church worshippers. Those involved in
emerging groups have gone with the mainline ecumenical flow in
affirming the value of set prayers and of classic shapes, patterns
and examples of prayer. This changed mindset allows a stance
of freedom and openness to the rich liturgical resources of other
traditions and other eras. In my experience, a renewed apprecia-
tion of and attentiveness to liturgical traditions among emerging
groups is more often rooted in what I would term a 'wisdom'
perspective, rather than a 'mandate' perspective, although some

would argue that such a dichotomy is artificial. By this I mean that most groups I know of do not have a 'singular' conception of 'the liturgy', and perceive themselves to have choices about how liturgy is shaped in a range of settings. (We will return to possible criticisms of this approach in the next chapter.) They are continually encountering 'old tricks', in terms of ancient forms of prayer and response that they find beautiful, enlightening and helpful. Having found them, they use them – sometimes in very conventional ways, sometimes in highly eclectic ways. Often, they use them without fully understanding the liturgical codes and conventions within which these 'old tricks' were previously embedded. Call this making it up as you go along, or call it anarchic liturgical *poiesis* – where it happens, those who disapprove or disdain it from the high church side of the equation have pastoral and personal choices here. They can simply condemn or sneer because by their lights, the liturgical glass is half-empty, or (even if they can't resist a wry smile or grimace) they can reckon the glass half-full and enter into a gracious conversation with those who are discovering the riches of 'their' tradition. I do not think that those options are spiritually or ethically equivalent for any believer and I continue to be angered and disappointed by the way 'liturgical fundamentalists' respond to the practice of emerging church groups.

Ritual action

The previous two observations, on the liturgical calendar and set forms and classic shapes, read the practice of alt/emerging groups as aligned rather closely with that of a range of mainline Protestant denominations. There is little here that goes beyond a common ecumenical evolution of interest and openness. In the area of ritual, however, emerging groups may have gone further and faster than most other Protestant congregations. (I deliberately speak in relative terms here, because my argument in most instances will not be that 'emerging' practices are either unique or unprecedented.) At the origins of alternative worship in the UK, there was a clear and rather conscious 'decision for the body' in worship.[41] One expression of this was an interest in ritual and ritual action. This was a dimension of liturgy that had almost completely dropped out of the repertoire of low church Protestants.[42] As well as the already largely made-safe rituals of lighting candles in worship, which were taken up ubiquitously and copiously by emerging groups, they began researching and using (not always in that order) rituals of anointing and censing. Some groups defied a still powerful taboo in most of their own backgrounds and 'retrieved' the action of making the sign of the cross and, at times, touching the cross. Many groups developed Ash Wednesday services (mainline Presbyterians, for example, are now widely observant of Lent in some way but still rarely hold a service to mark its beginning) which naturally included imposition of ashes. Postures for prayer became more diverse, with kneeling and standing both common. Many groups practised forms of the *asperges*: sprinkling or touching water as a reminder of baptism. Footwashing was widely practised, particularly in Maundy Thursday services, which also included variations on the 'stripping' of the worship space in preparation for Good Friday and its later refurbishment for Easter Day. The Easter Vigil, with the renewal of baptismal vows and kindling of new fire, was quickly taken up by many groups. Above all, these groups embraced '*the* action'; as Jason Byassee comments, 'It is hard to find one of these communities that does not celebrate the Eucharist more frequently than do its evangelical forebears.'[43] Byassee may be underplaying the frequency of some Baptist and Brethren celebrations, but in the round he is probably right. In the centring of worship around Eucharist, emerging groups have

41 See Jonny Baker and Doug Gay, *Alternative Worship*, London: SPCK/ Grand Rapids, MI: Baker, 2004, Introduction.

42 Although ritualized behaviour will always 'return' in even the contexts ostensibly most hostile to 'ritual'.

43 J. Byassee, 'Emerging from What, Going Where? Emerging Churches and Ancient Christianity', in Husbands and Greenman (eds), *Ancient Faith for the Church's Future*, p. 258.

again aligned their practice with the agenda of the Liturgical Movement.

Images and icons

One of the most distinctive and controversial features of the early alt worship services, which carried over into many emerging contexts, was the use of visual imagery. I will return to this in Chapter 4, because the representation of these images commonly involved non-traditional media; however, it also needs to be mentioned here, because so many of the images used were 'retrieved' from pre-modern worship settings. As with the retrieval of parts of older written liturgies, it was often the case that these images were represented in a disembodied and disembedded form – isolated both from their original setting and/or from their current physical setting in a church building, museum or art gallery. This raises many questions, most of which deserve to be addressed by someone more skilled in media studies/art history/aesthetics than I would claim to be. It does, though, deserve to be included within this account of the emerging practice of 'retrieval', and further reflection on the particular practices involved may in turn provoke new reflexive understandings and debates about a whole range of ways in which representation is (often unconsciously) practised within worship.

Spirituality and spiritual exercises

In the preface to a new edition of *The Wound of Knowledge*, Rowan Williams noted that the previous decade had seen 'something of an explosion of interest in and study of the history of Christian spirituality'.[44] Williams' beautifully observed historical study originally appeared just after Richard Foster's

---

44 Rowan Williams, *The Wound of Knowledge*, London: Darton, Longman and Todd, 1990 (1979), p. vii.

best-selling 1978 book *Celebration of Discipline* had 'crossed over' into the popular Christian market and introduced many low church and evangelical Christians for the first time to the vocabulary of 'spirituality' and 'spiritual disciplines'. Here was an already established wave of interest and exploration that was spreading beyond the sectors of the Church that had until now been stewards and 'directors' of this domain of the 'spiritual'. A new enthusiasm for 'Celtic spirituality' was also growing throughout the 1980s, popularized by writers such as Esther de Waal and David Adam. Again, this renewed interest in spirituality and spiritual exercises was understood self-consciously to be an act of retrieval. Just as the charismatic renewal had from the 1960s been in part a protest against and corrective to an overly textual and cerebral worship culture, so the renewal of interest in 'spirituality' had a parallel function in a contemplative mode. The influence of Taizé and Iona can also be seen here in the promotion by both of contemplative approaches to prayer, scripture and Christian devotion, and by Iona of a Celtic tradition of prayer and devotion. *Sojourners* magazine was another influence here from the 1970s, introducing new Christian publics to the work of Thomas Merton, Daniel Berrigan, Dorothy Day and others. All these and more helped to shape the strong interest among emerging groups in learning old tricks in this area.

Monasticism and spiritual 'rules'

In the mid twentieth century, the Taizé and Iona communities had been directly inspired by a broader ecumenical awakening of interest in monasticism. They were, if you like, along with the Catholic Worker Movement, the 'new monasticism' of the 1930s and 1940s and were particularly influenced by the ideals and rules of the Benedictine and Franciscan traditions.[45] Their

---

45 On the influence of Benedictine tradition on Iona, see Ralph Morton's fascinating book *Household of Faith*, Glasgow: Iona Community, 1951.

own appropriations and retrievals of these traditions took very different forms, but the CWM and both communities mediated their interest in them to a wider circle. Also beginning from the 1940s, the writings of Trappist monk Thomas Merton drew an ever wider readership and crossed over into liberal and then radical evangelical Protestant circles in subsequent decades.[46] It is interesting to note that an interest in monasticism has been a growing emphasis within the emerging conversation, coming to the fore more in the period from 2004 onwards than it was in the earlier alt/emerging years. Monasticism was, of course, another major low church taboo and a particular target of sixteenth-century Reformation polemics. Its rehabilitation is still a work in progress for many low church Protestants and its 'retrieval' is particularly subject to the kind of 'unbundling' we will discuss in the next chapter.

You'll take the low road

The main focus of this chapter has been on *low* church retrievals of *high* church tradition, but there is another stream that has fed the ecclesiology of the emerging project from a different direction. This might be better described as a low church retrieval of another 'deep' low church tradition. I mean by this the resurgence of interest since the 1970s in the traditions of the Radical Reformation, in the distinctive ecclesiologies of the Anabaptist/Believer's Church/Mennonite stream. The most widely read and discussed representative of this tradition is John Howard Yoder, whose 1972 book *The Politics of Jesus* represented an ecclesiological vision in which pacifism and non-violent resistance played an integral role. Yoder's work has been championed by Stanley Hauerwas among others, and Yoder (along with Karl Barth and a strange hybrid of John Paul II/Dorothy Day) was one of the 'three' exemplary Christian

---

46 *Seven Storey Mountain* was first published in 1948. *Sojourners* was and is, of course, a community before it is a magazine.

witnesses proposed by Hauerwas in his 2001 Gifford Lectures delivered in Scotland at the University of St Andrews.[47] Yoder's ecclesial vision is given a powerful expression in the brief book *Body Politics*,[48] a text that has been influential for some emerging groups. Another book that has played an analogous role in the emerging conversation more recently is Miroslav Volf's *After Our Likeness*, in which Volf performs a distinctive and powerful retrieval of the ecclesial thinking of the sixteenth-century English proto-Baptist John Smyth.[49] It is important to note that just as Hauerwas places Yoder in dialogue with Barth and John Paul II/Dorothy Day, so Volf places Smyth in dialogue with John Zizioulas and Joseph Ratzinger. Both are pointing to deficits in contemporary ecclesiology that call for the retrieval of this often neglected prophetic strand within the history of the Western churches – in Hauerwas' case, the deficit is primarily named in terms of peace and non-violence; in Volf's work, he audaciously uses Smyth to correct problematic understandings of 'catholicity'.

A final retrieval, which also belongs under this heading, would be the interest shown by some emerging groups in Quaker traditions of worship and non-violence. This can be related both to the previously mentioned interest in contemplative traditions of spirituality and to the interest in the witness of the 'peace churches' of the Radical Reformation.

Conclusion

I have argued in this chapter that *retrieval* is a key move and motif of the alt/emerging project. Using the broad rubrics of low and high church traditions, I have argued that the main

---

47 See note 22; Hauerwas' title is taken from John Howard Yoder's remark that 'people who carry crosses are going with the grain of the universe'.

48 Scottsdale, PA: Herald Press, 2001 (1992).

49 Grand Rapids, MI: Eerdmans, 1998.

trend within alt/emerging practice is towards a low church re-trieval of high church traditions, as groups seek to explore a deep/catholic dimension of their own ecclesial identities, par-ticularly in the area of worship and liturgy. I have also tried to display the extent to which there are many precedents and anticipations of this move, before and beyond the alt/emerg-ing conversation and to locate 'emerging church' in relation to larger trends towards retrieval and *ressourcement* within Western churches in the past 200 years. I have suggested that the Taizé and Iona communities have been key mediating in-stitutions for emerging groups. I have highlighted key areas in which the practice of emerging groups is marked by this move of retrieval, and given some concrete examples. Finally, I have noted some additional concerns to retrieve 'deep', 'low' church traditions.

I have emphasized the transgressive character of this move to retrieve 'catholic' (and radical Protestant) traditions and the extent to which many low church Protestants remained isolated from and ignorant of these traditions, prior to encountering and exploring them in 'emerging' settings. Having stressed the importance of retrieval to the hermeneutical ecclesiology of the emerging church project, I now want to reflect more closely on the kind of retrieval practised by emerging groups. To do that we need to propose a new hermeneutical move, explored in a new chapter.

3

'Tune My Heart to Sing Thy Grace'
Unbundling

The third move central to the emerging project I characterize as *unbundling*. I draw this rather clumsy term from the long-running dispute between Microsoft and the European Union over Microsoft's practice of bundling its proprietary internet browser with its operating system. The European Union opposed this as an anti-competitive practice and ruled that there should be an 'unbundling' of the two components.[1]

Reflecting on the practices of emerging church, this metaphor seemed to capture something crucial about the kind of retrieval that was being practised and to be worth isolating and considering as a distinct feature of the project. It could be seen as already contained within the movement of retrieval, but I think it deserves to be treated separately because it raises important theological questions about tradition and authority, freedom and order. It can perhaps be understood as a more reflective and deliberative move in contrast to the more playful, 'instinctive' and experimental mode in which retrieval seems often to take place.

Seen in this way, unbundling represents a move that pushes beyond the naivety of low church Protestant encounters with catholic tradition[2] and reflects more deeply on how to negotiate

---

1 http://en.wikipedia.org/wiki/European_Union_Microsoft_competi tion_case is as good a source as any for tracking this – with the usual caveats about a Wiki site.

2 In the emergers' defence, it can be said that a naive infatuation with catholic tradition can be readily noticed within various Presbyterian, Methodist and Episcopalian bodies from the nineteenth century onwards and still today – where the desire to ape (sometimes pre-Vatican II) Roman Catholic practice seems to be integral to clergy dressing up games and liturgical

the reception of practices and their accompanying theo-logics. This reflection is provoked by a realization (often visceral) that there are a good many low church 'import controls' still in place, in both institutionalized and internalized forms, which are simply not going to let certain things pass.

Above all, we are faced here with a rather messy set of theological negotiations regarding doctrines of church *order* and *ministry*: with how our churches recognize and authorize patterns of congregational (and denominational) life and ministry. The most controversial sites at which these negotiations are staged are around the celebration of the Lord's Supper/Eucharist/Holy Communion and the practice of Baptism.

Love/hate relationships

For many within the alt/emerging constituency there seems to be a common initial low church 'infatuation' with catholic sacramental practice. There is an excitement about encountering this richer and 'thicker' web of practices, entering a world filled with colour, gesture and symbolism and tapping into the deep veins of accompanying spirituality and devotional ethos. This encounter promises to recover a dimension of 'mystery' and 'transcendence' apparently lost within the practices of their own traditions. The difficulties arise when emerging groups reflect more fully on the way in which the practices they are drawn to and excited by are embedded within particular ecclesial structures and traditions, which continue to be concerned about policing and regulating those practices. The emergers realize, sometimes with a degree of shock and dismay, sometimes with a casual shrug of their shoulders, that the guardians of catholic tradition are fiercely committed to the principle that browser and operating system belong together in one 'bundle'.

'dances' with little desire to bring any critical insight to bear from within their own tradition: 'Dress me up as Mother and call me Father'!

Unbundling, of course, works in two directions simultaneously, since the low church groups negotiating a new relationship with/retrieval of catholic practice are also moving via the audit of their own traditions to unbundle packages of belief and practice that were often defended with equal conviction by the guardians of low church, 'evangelical' or 'reformed' bundles.

The crucial theological questions being asked of inherited bundles in each case have to do with how far linkages between belief, order and practice were theologically necessary and how far they reflect a range of historical, cultural and political contingencies that leave them open to reformulation (or even 'reformation'). This could be read as a description of the task of an *ecumenical* (practical) theology, which is how I would identify my own project here. My claim is that developing a hermeneutical ecclesiology through reflection on the practices of 'emerging' church opens up new possibilities for a deconstructive ecumenism.

The advent of the deconstructive Church

The Church: Emerging arrives as James K. A. Smith's 'deconstructive church' by way of a (non-linear) process of auditing, retrieval and unbundling. In the first chapter, I suggested that the idea of 'audit' prepared the way for this, noting Barth's powerful image of the present Christ dashing from our hands the claim to be identical with the true Church. Here in this deconstructive awareness of non-identity we can locate a weakening of confidence in the self-sufficiency of low church traditions, which creates an appetite for retrieval (and also shapes the 'supplementing' we explore in the next chapter). This is bound up with a new set of possibilities for critiquing low church traditions, especially charismatic/evangelical ones, in terms of their ambitions to be culturally 'modernizing'. This postmodern critique of church cultures and sub cultures[3]

---

3 See Pete Ward's description of the church as a fluid 'taste culture' in *Participation and Mediation*, London: SCM Press, 2008, p. 176.

creates a new openness to the Church's past traditions of practice, including pre-modern and pre-Reformation traditions.

However, such deconstructive sensibilities do not only operate in relation to low church origins; they are also in play within the process of retrieval itself, because they are equally applied to the claims of 'higher' traditions. No past, 'low' or 'high', Protestant, Catholic or Orthodox, is seen to be immune from critique or able to hold fast in its own hands a claim to complete identity with the true Church. The critique of patriarchy, for example, is one of a number of cross-cutting theological imperatives that indict all available traditions, as are critiques of affluence, power and violence. Low church Protestants are in any case instinctively or habitually suspicious of strong claims to authority from high traditions and do not lose this overnight simply because they became more critical of their own home base.

The result is, therefore, that the advent of the deconstructive church sees the emergence of Christians conscious of deficiencies in their own low traditions, who aim to remedy this, not by simple conversion or submission, but by binding the strong men and plundering their goods. The process of retrieval is, in other words, to be highly selective. There is to be, in that overused but not useless characterization of postmodernity, a pick'n'mix approach. There is a sense in which, to paraphrase the imagery of Matthew 13.52, catholic tradition is to be approached as a kind of massive dressing-up box, a huge CD collection, a sprawling image bank, a compendium of stage directions, a liturgical lending library.

The justification for this lies in a recognition that, as Daniel Williams says, 'the Christian tradition was and always is in the process of development' and that 'in itself there is nothing sacrosanct about tradition'.[4] In the sense that it is a 'source', therefore, to adapt an album title from the late great Scottish singer-songwriter John Martyn, tradition is a source of both

---

4 D. H. Williams, *Evangelicals and Tradition: The Formative Influence of the Early Church*, Grand Rapids, MI: Baker Academic, 2005, pp. 8,18.

grace and danger. To accept this is to confess that Christian tradition both contains old mistakes and achieves new clarifications.[5] The clearest and most significant example of this must be the recognition, after almost two millennia of Christian history, of the theological case for the ordination of women. The persistence within church tradition of a patriarchal prohibition on women's ordination for such an extended period is one of the most compelling arguments in favour of relativizing the authority of tradition and magisterium.

The possibility therefore arises here that some of the fiercest criticism of 'emerging church' (and there has been plenty) relates not just to its excesses and follies (of which there are also plenty) but to the fundamental theological arguments it has engaged on both 'left' and 'right', 'low' and 'high' wings of the ecclesiological debate. There is a double transgression at work here, which provokes a double critique and leads to the emerging conversation being squeezed from both sides. To the low/left, emergers are catholic wannabes; to the high/right, they are Protestant dilettantes. So both sides of the vice squeezing the emerging practitioners might agree in the verdict that the objects of their critique are innocents abroad.

One of my aims in writing this book is to try to name and narrate something of the theological difficulty that the emerging project finds itself in and to do so with as much generosity and sympathy as I can muster towards all sides, in the hope that this will enable both critics and 'emergers' to better understand one another's positions.

In the rest of this chapter I first set out some concrete examples of 'unbundling' in practice and then develop a theological reflection on what is at stake in 'unbundling'. This reflection draws on three key theological resources: Jürgen Moltmann's concept of apostolic procession; Miroslav Volf's

---

5 'The Lord had more truth and light yet to break forth out of his holy Word.' Words of John Robinson's final address to the pilgrims upon their departure to the New World, 1620, as told by Governor Edward Winslow in *Hypocrisie Unmasked*, 1646.

radical reformation articulation of catholicity; and Lamin Sanneh's work on translation, as well as my own critical reading of Prosper of Aquitaine's (in)famous dictum, *lex orandi statuat lex credendi*.

Unbundled practice

Unbundling is not new. The history of the Church contains both dramatic and notorious examples. Arguably the two greatest of these are the beginnings of the Gentile churches in the first century AD and the Protestant Reformation(s) in the sixteenth century. In both cases we find strong elements of continuity in relation to belief and practice, but also a reforming refusal of pressure to swallow whole an existing package of church life and a conviction that faithfulness to the gospel and openness to the Spirit required the Church to change, even at the cost of schism and division.

Not all examples of unbundling within the practice of emerging groups are theologically or ecumenically equal. In some cases the retrieval or borrowing from another tradition simply involves a practice that is unfamiliar among low church Protestants but is subject to no real export or import controls from either side of the exchange. In cases like this, a practice is unbundled from its usual context, but there is no great theological principle held to be at stake in its appropriation or reception. The language of gift and sharing is most likely to accompany such exchanges, which represent one end of a spectrum of responses to retrieval. At the other end of that spectrum lies the type of appropriation that is viewed with suspicion, distaste or even horror by those insiders who perceive the authority or integrity of their tradition to have been breached.

For the examples offered here it is not possible to map them definitively on such a spectrum, because different groups and 'authorities' would use different calibrations of catholic tradition to assess them. It is important, however, for an ecumenical theology to demonstrate its awareness that such a spectrum of affirmation and offence exists and that it forms a backdrop to assessments of the identity and practices of emerging groups.

Example 1 – Ash Wednesday

An emerging congregation based within a 'reformed' congregation holds an Ash Wednesday service. Their service follows an Anglican liturgical text, but the imposition of ashes takes place on lines adapted from the Iona Abbey Healing Service.[6] One lay person leads the prayers before the imposition of ashes, another two move round a circle of those who have come forward and knelt to receive the marking and with it the charge: *'Remember you are dust and to dust you shall return; turn away from your sins and be faithful to Christ.'*

Reflecting on this example of practice, there are multiple layers of retrieval present: an early medieval Roman Catholic practice[7] is being retrieved through the filter of a twentieth-century Anglican text (itself a retrieval since the Church of England banned the practice in 1548). There is also unbundling going on, however, since most people who have experienced such a service are only ever likely to have been 'ashed' by a Roman Catholic priest or an Anglican vicar. Here the emerging/reformed reception of the practice unbundles both the ritual and the text from the previous clerical monopoly and opens the liturgical voice and action to 'lay' actors. Although it is being retrieved into an emerging context which recognizes the role of ordained ministers, there is no sense here of needing to assimilate this retrieved practice to the set of practices reserved to an ordained Reformed minister.

---

6 The Healing Service is available as an e-Liturgy download from Wild Goose Publications at www.ionabooks.com/PL10006-Healing-Service-Iona-Abbey.html.

7 So Joanne Pierce, 'Ash Wednesday', in Paul Bradshaw (ed.), *The New SCM Dictionary of Liturgy and Worship*, London: SCM Press, 2006, p. 30.

There is, therefore, a multiple unbundling at work, but while it might puzzle Roman and Anglo-Catholics, this particular ritual occupies something of a grey area. Distribution of ashes is not a sacrament and the words spoken are words of exhortation, which do not intrinsically seem to require an ordained voice behind them. The 'host' traditions for this ritual might not think of devolving it to the laity, but they also might not be utterly scandalized by that happening in another context.[8]

Example Two – Congregational 'presidency'

An independent emerging congregation holds a communion service. In contrast to the low church Protestant background of most worshippers, the liturgy follows a classic high shape and includes the *Gloria, Kyrie eleison, Benedictus, Agnus Dei,* Apostles' Creed and the Lord's Prayer. The Eucharistic Prayer is shared by male and female voices (both lay) and includes an *epiclesis* voiced in unison by the whole congregation, before the elements are broken/poured and lifted high by the male and female laypeople.

Here again we clearly have retrieval, rooted in a strong 'liturgical literacy', but we also have unbundling, which is seen in the appropriation and editing/splicing/revoicing of liturgical texts in novel ways. Here, too, we find an example of practice very likely to cause offence to mainline denominations. It does, however, represent an unusual example of the 'trangressions' involved. Those traditions that advocate and practise 'lay presidency' tend to bundle that practice with a 'low' attitude towards liturgical tradition and to eschew the use of classic texts

---

8 A similar example might be the 'Benediction' or 'Blessing of the People' – an action reserved to priests in Roman and Anglican traditions and restricted to Ministers of Word and Sacrament by some Presbyterians. The practice is already unbundled in orders such as those in Iona's *Wee Worship Book* by being turned into 'closing responses' shared between a (lay) lead voice and shared voices. Although formal/official positions on this (to me theologically baffling) monopoly show little sign of change, unbundling this practice from ordained status is unlikely to provoke fierce opposition.

(or indeed any set texts) and prayers from Catholic tradition. 'High' liturgical traditions, on the other hand, resolutely refuse to countenance what they would call 'lay presidency'. The distinctive liturgical and textual habits of 'high' and 'low' are always tightly bundled with their respective attitudes towards church order and 'presidency'. What is different about this instance of emerging practice (and it is representative rather than typical) is that it scrambles the high/low distinction by its twin interest in retrieval and unbundling. Its 'hybrid' liturgical style is transgressive, disconcerting and deconstructive.

Justifying unbundling

The arguments for and against such unbundlings display classic fault lines of Christian disagreement in relation to authority and order. Without underestimating the theological difficulty of addressing such hardened ecumenical stand-offs, I want to explore the kind of theological resources that might help to justify practices of unbundling, or at least to make them more intelligible to their critics. I hope that they may also address questions of the self-understanding of the Church: Emerging, and in particular how it understands itself in relation to the classic ecclesiological 'marks' of unity, holiness, catholicity and apostolicity.

Apostolic procession

Questions of authority within the Church are intimately bound up with questions of apostolicity. For many low church Protestants, apostolicity has been absorbed without remainder into their doctrine of scripture and their doctrine of the Holy Spirit, with these authorities immediately available to all people at all times, in ways that could be fully constitutive of ecclesiality. Within higher traditions, however, the doctrine of *apostolic succession* has had a fundamental role in shaping understandings of church order, valid ordination and valid sacraments; in fact, the basic conditions of ecclesiality, of being a 'church', turn on this for the Roman Catholic Church. This was reiterated in the notorious *Responses to some Questions Regarding Certain Aspects of the Doctrine on the Church*, released by the Congregation for the Doctrine of the Faith in June 2007. The document states in response to a direct question about the ecclesiality of the 'Christian Communities' (sic) born out of the sixteenth-century Reformation: 'According to Catholic doctrine, these Communities do not enjoy apostolic succession in the sacrament of Orders, and are, therefore, deprived of a constitutive element of the Church.'[9]

This document, although in many ways predictable and unexceptional, still caused grave offence to millions of Protestants by the fact of its production. It offers the classic Roman insistence on bundling practice and order, carried through to the logical but ecumenically disastrous outcome of denying the full ecclesiality of all other Christian churches. Much to the pain and dismay of (particularly higher) Anglicans, it continues to class them among the ecclesiologically deprived.[10] However, the briefest of readings of the history of ecumenical dialogue in the twentieth and twenty-first centuries shows the tendency of Anglicans to repeat the same verdict in relation to other (non-episcopal) churches. Anglicans have unbundled episcopacy from Rome, but they have not (yet) unbundled ordination or confirmation from episcopacy. While they take a softer line on recognition of the ecclesiality of other churches, their continuing official articulations of apostolic succession still tend towards a lack of recognition of the order of other denominations.

---

9 www.vatican.va/roman_curia/congregations/cfaith/documents/rc_con_cfaith_doc_20070629_responsa-quaestiones_en.html.

10 The more recent creation of an Anglican 'ordinariate' moves this situation on without materially changing the basic position in terms of recognizing ecclesiality. www.vatican.va/holy_father/benedict_xvi/apost_constitutions/documents/hf_benxvi_apc_20091104_anglicanorum-coetibus_en.html.

As yet there is no way to align these understandings of apostolic succession with one another or with the understandings of apostolicity/apostolic authority current among low church Protestants. Perhaps the best that can be achieved within ecumenical theology at present is the continuing attempt to understand and explain one's own position as clearly as possible in dialogue with others and to understand other positions in dialogue with those who hold them.

It would be hard not to credit Jürgen Moltmann with being an ecumenical theologian and I believe that an ecclesiology open to 'emerging' insights can be helped by his work. In particular, Moltmann's undervalued ecclesiological classic *The Church in the Power of the Holy Spirit* makes a powerful case for a reforming perspective on tradition. Perhaps the most important theological proposal Moltmann makes in this book is that we should opt to speak of *apostolic procession* alongside apostolic succession.[11] The idea of procession is a fruitful one because it has the potential to recognize the authority of origins, along with patterns of connection and continuity, but without imposing the same kind of theological closure on ecclesiology that has made apostolic succession too much a rationale for *apostolic exclusion*.[12] It is also highly compatible with a strong understanding of apostolic authority being mediated through scripture, while offering a constructive language for engaging ecumenical debates. An emerging ecclesiology could therefore draw on Moltmann's proposal as a key resource for understanding and expressing its own apostolicity.[13]

---

11 London: SCM Press, 1977, pp. 312ff.; for an important recent appropriation of this term within ecumenical dialogue (in the context of debates around women becoming bishops) see the response to Walter Kasper's June 2006 paper to the Church of England's House of Bishops, written by N. T. Wright and David Stancliffe. Available at: www.fulcrum-anglican.org.uk/news/2006/20060721kasper.cfm?doc=126 (accessed 1 June 2009).

12 See Miroslav Volf, *After Our Likeness*, Grand Rapids, MI: Eerdmans, 1998, p. 260.

13 I recognize that some emerging groups remain within churches that uphold apostolic succession but I hope that this proposal remains valuable

Radically reformed catholicity

Moving to the 'mark' of *catholicity*, one of Moltmann's former students, the Croatian Baptist Miroslav Volf, presented a remarkable ecumenical reworking of Radical Reformation ecclesiology in *After Our Likeness*.[14] On the one hand, Volf draws attention to the 'growing congregationalization' of traditional Protestant *and* Catholic churches[15] and suggests that:

> Today's global developments seem to imply that Protestant Christendom of the future will largely exhibit a Free Christian form . . . It seems clear to me that we are standing in the middle of a clear and irreversible 'process of congregation-alization'.[16]

However, he also warns: 'If the Free Churches want to contribute to the salvation of Christendom, they themselves must first be healed.'[17] This will involve these churches converting their 'protest' identities into 'an ecclesiological program' and doing so by entering into a serious ecumenical dialogue with Catholic and Orthodox ecclesiologies.[18] Volf moves to do just this by staging a highly original and unprecedented trialogue between Joseph Ratzinger,[19] John Zizioulas[20] and the sixteenth-century English Baptist John Smyth.[21] A crucial feature of Volf's defence of the true ecclesiality of free churches is his articulation of the meaning of catholicity in terms of 'the *openness* of

---

for them in terms of recognition of other groups located beyond episcopal traditions.

14 Volf, *After Our Likeness*, 1998.

15 Volf, *After Our Likeness*, p. 12.

16 Volf, *After Our Likeness*, pp. 12, 13.

17 Volf, *After Our Likeness*, p. 18.

18 Volf, *After Our Likeness*, p. 11.

19 Now Pope Benedict XVI.

20 A former lecturer at my own University of Glasgow and now Eastern Orthodox Metropolitan of Pergamon.

21 The audacity of Volf's choice for the third dialogue partner makes this a truly original and fascinating book.

every church toward all other churches'.[22] Within such a revised understanding of catholicity, he argues that 'the ecclesiality of a local church need not depend on the sacramental relation to [all other churches]'.[23] Volf's work has been much discussed in alt/emerging circles and there is a case to be made that the emerging conversation is itself a useful example of the kind of inter-ecclesial openness he is calling for. The emphasis on retrieval involves a diachronic openness to the riches of the communion of churches from Pentecost to Constantinople, from Geneva to Azusa Street and beyond. The emphasis on supplementing, which we shall explore further in the next chapter, can be understood in relation to Volf's stress on the need for synchronic openness to today's global communion of churches. An emerging ecclesiology could therefore draw on Volf's proposal as a key resource for understanding its own catholicity and through this, its own ecclesiality. But perhaps it can also do more than this. In the Introduction to *After Our Likeness*, Volf ventures the suggestion that: 'Insofar as the ecclesiology of the Free Churches becomes ecumenically plausible, it can perhaps also function as a catalyst in the search for a postconfessional ecumenical conceptual framework.'[24] While stressing once more my recognition that not all emerging churches are 'free churches', I believe it is possible that the emerging ecclesiological journey has helped some groups to display something of that ecumenical plausibility Volf is envisioning. If so, they can aspire to be part of a solution: part of the healing of both the introversion of free church ecclesiology and the exclusivity of Catholic and Orthodox ecclesiology. For an individual church to say this might sound like hubris, but if there is any plausibility to my attempt to reflect on some wider common moves within the Church: Emerging, perhaps the claim is at least worthy of discussion in the spirit of inter-ecclesial open-

22 Volf, *After Our Likeness*, p. 156. Volf speaks of a diachronic [historical] and synchronic [contemporary] openness to the communion of churches within history: pp. 156, 158.
23 Volf, *After Our Likeness*, p. 156.
24 Volf, *After Our Likeness*, p. 21.

ness that Volf commends. Certainly some such revised open understanding of catholicity is also necessary if Stanley Hauerwas' vision of a church open to Barth, Yoder and John Paul II is to have any chance of a 'concrete instantiation'.[25]

Cultural translation

Another significant resource for thinking the concept of 'unbundling' is found in the work of the missiologist, cultural theorist and church historian Lamin Sanneh. In Sanneh's groundbreaking missiological work *Translating the Message* he argues that the metaphor and practices of *translation* are crucial to understanding the historical development of Christian practice. Christian practice is always already experienced and received as inculturated practice, and within the *missio Dei* the further transmission of the gospel and the birth of new Christian communities is predicated on practices of cultural translation. Sanneh observes that:

> It seems to be part of the earliest records we possess that the disciples came to a clear and firm position regarding the translatability of the gospel, with a commitment to the pluralist merit of culture within God's universal purpose.[26]

He expands on this by arguing that:

> Christianity is first and foremost a pluralist religion . . . As Paul affirmed, there is no respect of persons with God (Rom

---

25 Hauerwas sometimes describes himself as a 'high-church Mennonite'. For Hauerwas' trio of witnesses see *With the Grain of the Universe*, Grand Rapids, MI: Brazos/London: SCM Press, 2001; for a self-deprecating reference to the 'concrete instantiation' of Hauerwas' vision of church, see *Performing the Faith*, London: Grand Rapids, MI: Baker Academic/London: SPCK, 2004; on Barth and 'catholicity' see Chapter 5 of Reinhard Hutter's *Bound to be Free*, Grand Rapids, MI: Eerdmans, 2004.

26 L. Sanneh, *Translating the Message*, Maryknoll, NY: Orbis, 1989, p. 1.

2:11) and nothing in itself is unclean (Rom 14:14). The positive sides of these statements are equally valid: all persons are precious in God's sight (1 Pet 2:4) and all things indeed are pure (Rom 14:20). In the same fashion, no one is the exclusive or normative pattern for anyone else and no one culture can be God's favourite. The result is pluralism on a radical scale, one that even institutional Christianity finds it difficult to accept or promote. But if translatability is the taproot of Christian expansion, then resistance to it by ecclesiastical institutions is like the rebellion of the branches against the tree . . . Mission helps to burst the old wineskins with the pressure of cross-cultural interpretation, dissolving the barriers of cultural exclusiveness.[27]

For Sanneh, the practices of translation force a distinction between the essence of the message and its cultural presuppositions:

Thus, mission as translation makes the bold, fundamental assertion that the recipient culture is the authentic destination of God's salvific promise and as a consequence, has an honored place under the 'kindness of God' . . . By drawing a distinction between the message and its surrogate, mission as translation affirms the *missio Dei* as the hidden force for its work.[28]

Sanneh's work is also important for the discussion of *supplementing*, which we will move to in the next chapter, but here I want to consider its significance for unbundling. From its beginnings, the alt worship and emerging church conversations have been attentive to and influenced by the literature

---

27 Sanneh, *Translating the Message*, p. 30.
28 Sanneh, *Translating the Message*, p. 31. Many other missiologists have done crucial work on questions of 'inculturation' and 'contextualization'. I focus on Sanneh's work because I think it is a particularly bold and far-reaching reflection on the issues at stake.

of missiology.[29] This connection was driven by the recognition that their revisions of worship practice were crossing cultural boundaries within postmodern, media-saturated Western societies. What the alt/emerging practitioners learned from missiology was how to reflect on the ways in which inherited bundles of church practice, while they were defended and serviced by means of supposedly pure theo-logics, were invariably shaped by cultural and contextual factors. Within the history of Christian missions, this inculturation of practice had often been concealed and denied. This blindness to inculturation took place, as the prayer of confession says, 'through ignorance, through weakness and through our own deliberate fault'. Whether knowingly or unknowingly, whether as sin of omission or of commission, the failure to perceive how cultural factors always influence and shape the bundling of Christian practice and its theo-logics was itself a practice of domination. One of Sanneh's most telling insights relates to the way in which the results of the practice of translation, even when it was instigated by dominant, imperialist and colonialist parties, carry an ironic and subversive power to escape the control of the translators and empower indigenous, 'missionized' peoples.[30]

Unbundling, therefore, also calls for an active missiological intelligence to be at work in reflecting on the Church's practice. Here, Pete Ward's recent call for Practical Theology to develop an active dialogue with cultural studies is of real importance.[31] Questions of worship and liturgy, which have been to the forefront of this book's concerns, have historically been particularly prone to culture-blindness. Both within individual denominations and within trans-denominational movements like evangelicalism, theological rationalizations have been used to effectively absolutize cultural/aesthetic choices. These rationalizations tend to work in one of two ways. Either there is

---

29 See Chapter 2 of Pete Ward's *Participation and Mediation* for his explanation of the importance of missiological literature on his theological development.

30 Sanneh, *Translating the Message*, pp. 53ff.

31 Ward, *Participation and Mediation*, p. 12.

a 'docetic' tendency to deny or conceal inculturation (this ignores the gin-and-tonic rule of Christian practice, which states that we never get the Holy Spirit neat; there is always a cultural mixer) or there is an ethnocentric tendency to falsely privilege one mode of inculturation over others. The issue here is not that one mode of inculturation will always be privileged in any given situation (that is unavoidable); it is a failure to understand the status of 'our' inculturated practice and an inability to accompany our practice with theological reflection. I therefore strongly support Pete Ward's view that:

> For the ministerial professional who is engaged in the expression of faith in the Emerging Church or among young people, or within migrant communities, mission studies as a conversation around culture and theology is a vital resource, not least because it is in cross-cultural mission that our own cultural, ecclesial and theological norms are seen to be relativized.[32]

Both Ward and Timothy Gorringe[33] offer an important corrective to tendencies within the Radical Orthodoxy (RO) collective in this area. Particularly in the work of John Milbank, which I otherwise greatly admire, there are ethnocentric, anglocentric (and Anglican-centric) tendencies that surface in judgements about contemporary liturgy and ecclesiology.[34] It is as if, having accomplished so much philosophical heavy lifting on behalf of contemporary theology, they assume their own aesthetic and cultural instincts to be perfectly calibrated in

---

32 Ward, *Participation and Mediation* p. 59.

33 T. Gorringe, *Furthering Humanity: A Theology of Culture*, Aldershot, Ashgate, 2004.

34 The worst 'topical' example here is John Milbank's seriously misjudged, poorly informed and frankly snobbish piece, 'Stale Expressions: The Management Shaped Church', *Studies in Christian Ethics*, 21:1 (2008), pp. 117–28. Of the founding trinity, Graham Ward's work displays by far the soundest instincts for and the most rounded awareness of popular culture.

respect of judging and evaluating church practice. I suspect that at least some within RO circles regard missiology as rather beneath them, but I believe they and other 'systematic' or 'philosophical' theologians who take this stance do so to their own impoverishment.

Some readers may be choking with indignation that such judgements can be offered from a perspective sympathetic to the emerging conversation, since emerging groups have often been accused of a facile and superficial concern for 'style' and 'cool worship'. While there is doubtless some truth in that objection, I want to argue that at their best, many emerging groups have been extremely thoughtful and self-critical about their own practice. They have been attentive to missiology and to the harsh lessons taught to Western churches by the often excoriating post-colonial debriefing of the past practice of Western missions. This attentiveness has been born of their experience of cross-cultural mission *within* Western societies and the self-questioning it provoked about their own practice.[35] In my own case, the early days of my involvement in the alternative worship movement in Scotland coincided with my first ten weeks of theological study, which were taught by Lesslie Newbigin, then the visiting Alexander Robertson Lecturer at the University of Glasgow. Newbigin's 1988 lectures to us, subsequently published as *The Gospel in a Pluralist Society*,[36] and the work of the 'Gospel and Our Culture Network' in which he was a leading figure, emphasized the challenge faced by Western churches in developing a missiological reading of Western culture.[37]

---

35 It is significant that one of the leading UK networkers and reflectors on emerging church, Jonny Baker, works for the Church Missionary Society (CMS) of the Church of England.

36 London: SPCK, 1989.

37 On this see also David Bosch's short book *Believing in the Future: Toward a Missiology of Western Culture*, Valley Forge, PA: Trinity Press International, 1995; also Kevin J. Vanhoozer, Charles A. Anderson, Michael J. Sleasman (eds), *Everyday Theology: How to Read Cultural Texts and Interpret Trends*, Grand Rapids, MI: Baker Academic, 2007.

The emerging church conversation, therefore, to the degree that it has been attentive to such missiological concerns, has been able to develop some acute theological instincts for questioning the cultural bundling of ecclesial practice. This is significant because despite the advances made at Vatican II,[38] such instincts remain underdeveloped within Western churches. The insights and lessons of missiology are a key resource for the revision of Christian practice in the twenty-first century. Attending to them is a task that belongs at the heart of theological reflection and, as Geoffrey Wainwright suggests, belongs to the very definition of a living and growing Christian tradition:

> Christian theology requires a *religious canon* (specifically the apostolic faith, which defines historic Christianity and includes a confession of the unique and universal significance of Jesus Christ) and allows a *cultural pluralism* (as part of an ecclesial catholicity in time and space that allows grace to transform rather than destroy culture). The concept and reality that join these two together is that of an *assimilative tradition*.[39]

One of the most widely cited theological statements in this area has been the 1996 Nairobi Statement, *On Worship and Culture: Contemporary Challenges and Opportunities*, which was the product of a study process of the World Lutheran Federation.[40] The Nairobi Statement offers useful reflections on the value of analysing relationships between culture and Christian practice in terms of their transcultural, contextual, counter-cultural and cross-cultural dynamics.[41] It is not a perfect statement (the work of Pete Ward and Timothy Gorringe, among others, points to ways in which its categories need to be refined) but it is a helpful

---

38 See the 1988 *Missal for the Dioceses of Zaire*, cited in Geoffrey Wainwright, *Worship with One Accord: Where Liturgy and Ecumenism Embrace*, New York: Oxford University Press, 1997, p. 263.

39 Wainwright, *Worship with One Accord*, p. 264.

40 Available at www.worship.ca/docs/lwf_ns.html (accessed 2 June 2009).

41 Nairobi Statement, 1.3ff.

one, and one that is born out of a post-colonial attempt to develop a global dialogue about church practice. What we can trace here, therefore, is a developing ecumenical awareness of the need for cultural unbundling within denominational traditions of practice. This relates both to the ways in which denominational traditions of practice (including Roman traditions) are marked and limited by their ethnic origins and sojourns and also to the ways in which they are marked and limited by their class locations and origins. My argument has been that this awareness has been fitfully and partially, but nonetheless really, present within the emerging conversation. Here again, Barth's image applies – the truly present Christ dashes from the hands of every *KulturKirche* (and every church is a 'culture church') the claim to be identical with the one true Church.

Conclusion

A further comment by Geoffrey Wainwright helpfully brings together the three emphases explored above:

> The *regula fidei* [rule of faith] is self-referential in confessing a church that is 'holy, catholic and apostolic'. A church that abides by the apostolic norm will display its catholicity by including in its life those features from the variety of human cultures that prove marked or markable by the holiness revealed in the person and work of Jesus Christ and released in abundance by the Pentecostal outpouring of the Holy Spirit. It is the observance of the apostolic norm that prevents syncretism in the sense of adulteration.[42]

In this chapter, as throughout the book, I have been trying to show that the key hermeneutical moves made by the Church: Emerging are not unprecedented and that they can be fruitfully

---

42 Wainwright, *Worship with One Accord*, p. 269.

understood in relation to a broader series of ecumenical conversations about the Church, its worship and mission. In one final cross-reference, I want to suggest that the metaphor of unbundling can be read against the backdrop of ecumenical debates over the meaning of *lex orandi, lex credendi* (law of prayer, law of belief). In his systematic theology *Doxology*, Geoffrey Wainwright noted that it was unusual for this theme to be taken up by Protestant writers, and observed that:

> from the grammatical point of view it is equally possible to reverse subject and predicate and so take the tag as meaning that the rule of faith is the norm of prayer: what must be believed governs what may and should be prayed. The linguistic ambiguity of the Latin tag corresponds to a material interplay which in fact takes place between worship and doctrine in Christian practice: worship influences doctrine and doctrine worship.[43]

In a sustained discussion over two chapters, Wainwright points out the tendency for Protestant and Catholic thinkers to read the phrase in opposite directions, with Catholics more characteristically appealing to liturgical practice as a basis for doctrinal formulation and Protestants favouring the role of doctrine in critiquing and controlling liturgical practice.[44] Scottish practical theologian Duncan Forrester discusses the phrase in an article in which he joins Wainwright in registering Protestant reserve over assertions of the priority of prayer over belief, arguing instead for a necessary dialectic between the two.[45] The unbundling moves of the emerging project can be seen as examples of such a dialectical reading of *lex orandi, lex credendi*, although here, as before, we can anticipate the criticism that it fails to properly make either *lex rex*.

---

43 Geoffrey Wainwright, *Doxology*, New York: Oxford University Press, 1980, p. 218.

44 Wainwright, *Doxology*, pp. 251ff.

45 Duncan Forrester, 'Lex Orandi, Lex Credendi', in Duncan Forrester (ed.), *Theology and Praxis*, London: Epworth, 1990, p. 79.

This has been the hardest chapter of this book to write and may be the one that provokes most criticism. I am all too aware of the ways in which it treads on both thin ice and holy ground[46] in attempting to describe how the emerging conversation is re-negotiating understandings of tradition and authority within the Church. That conversation has much to gain from deepening its liturgical and ecumenical literacy, not least through the services of a wise and patient ecumenical scholar and activist like Wainwright. But I dare to hope and suggest that broader ecumenical/liturgical conversations might also have things to gain from welcoming the upstart newcomers of 'emerging church' into their debates. In an era when ecumenism has been in danger of becoming a theological 'geek' topic for many and its achievements on the ground have looked painfully thin, the anarchic explorations of emerging practice have generated waves of excitement and interest around some central ecumenical themes. This contrast is worth reflecting on.

Finally, I want to consider a powerful contribution to this discussion made by D. Stephen Long in a symposium honouring the work of Robert Webber, held at Wheaton College in 2007. Long's contribution, entitled 'Two Augustinianisms: Augustinian Realism and the Other City', moves from its exploration of Augustinian readings of ecclesial and political community to a conclusion that puts a profound question to the emerging church conversation and its embrace of Webber's ancient-future vision:

> How can we have a truly catholic unity based on a common worship and life, drawing on the ancients, leading us into the future unity we know Christ seeks for his church?
>
> At least these two possibilities emerge. First we might find our way back to Rome as communions (not individuals). We will need to live in such a way that Catholics see our faith and seek a genuine unity. We will also need their ecclesial

---

46 Despite the mixed metaphor, these indeed may sometimes be one and the same.

structures, for they have had the only successful transnational unity grounded in a penitential structure that did not finally depend on a modern nation-state or ethnic identity for its viability. Second, we could work toward a conciliar Catholicism, which forges a common penitential structure that would include accountability in doctrine, worship and life, perhaps along the lines of the newly developing Anglican covenant. Without some such politics of sameness that unites us in the one body of Christ and asks of us obedience to something other than ourselves, then I fear that what will emerge in recent evangelical efforts to recover antiquity for the future of the church will be nothing but one more consumer option we individuals can choose to give our lives meaning. And that will be about as significant as the food court at the mall. If the emergent movement contributes to this transnational unity, it will be truly emergent and we pray God's blessings on it. If it only seeks to be one more consumer option further fragmenting Christ's already fragmented, tortured body, then may it go the way of other commodity fetishes like Pokemon cards and hula hoops. I hope and pray it will be the former.[47]

Long's question deserves serious consideration by all of us within the emerging conversation and I am grateful for it. The move of unbundling, in particular, runs a high risk of falling over into a consumerist evasion of responsibility for seeking the peace and unity of the Church. That said, as we have noted above, the inherited tight authoritarian bundles of existing traditions have done their own kind of damage to catholic unity and Christian mission. As Volf has suggested, the shapes and habits acquired by twentieth-century ecumenism can seem profoundly inhospitable to a global Church that is experiencing rapid 'congregationalization' and within which evangelical,

---

47 D. Stephen Long in M. Husbands and J. P. Greenman (eds), *Ancient Faith for the Church's Future*, Downers Grove, IL: InterVarsity Press, 2008, pp. 244, 245.

Pentecostal and 'free church' traditions are increasing in size and significance. The Church: Emerging may yet be a hopeful bridge between a Protestantism too careless of its catholicity and a 'catholicism/orthodoxy' that has too often fetishized its own apostolicity.

4

'Always Being Reformed'
Supplementing

Not everything the Church needs for its existence in the world is already there within the tradition. The nature of the Church's pilgrimage as a journey through space and time involves it in a continuing negotiation between the faith once delivered to the saints and the incarnation of that faith in each new context. This truth is so basic to the Church's existence that it should not need to be pressed or laboured, but the history of the Church in every time and place bears witness to the pain and resistance that accompany change. The Church often finds change hard and often gets it wrong. More than that, it is a central premise of the argument of this book and of a hermeneutical ecclesiology that it never gets it entirely right. There is always something forgotten that can be remembered and something not yet learned that can be discovered. The principle of *semper reformanda* is therefore both an entirely right and entirely necessary expression of the Church's epistemic and hermeneutical humility.

In exploring the fourth move, of *supplementing*, we are concerned with the renewal of the Church and the ways in which this involves what the Second Vatican Council described as *aggiornamento* – originally used to refer to 'adjournment' of Canon Law, but usually translated as 'updating'. (There are good reasons why we are unlikely to see a publisher developing a book series called *Evangelical Aggiornamento*,[1] reflecting the fact that Protestants have been notorious for this since the sixteenth-century Reformation.)

The emerging church conversation is known for and by its commitment to supplementing as well as retrieval. In this

---

1 See the Baker Academic series *Evangelical Ressourcement*.

chapter I explore six key supplements to ecclesiology, which have been inherited, practised and championed by emerging groups. By a supplement, I mean something that is a significant addition or innovation to existing church practice, that has not previously existed in the same form within church tradition. As always, I want to qualify the account given here by recognizing that most of these supplements are not at all unique to the emerging conversation, nor are all groups associated with that conversation equally enamoured of or involved with them; nor do all groups deploy the same theo-logics in the way they understand and incorporate them into their practice. It is the concentration and layering of these features within the discourse and practice of emerging groups that justifies them being considered as characteristic or identifying.

Ecumenism

I have already drawn attention to connections and relations between the terms 'emerging' and 'ecumenical', and I will return to this in the final chapter. Here I want to conceive of ecumenism as itself a supplement in the sense of its diffusive influence on the emerging conversation. Emerging groups are rarely formal actors in ecumenical processes, and rarely talk the language of 'ecumenism', but they have absorbed the influence of the Ecumenical Movement in the form of a generalized respect for and interest in a wide range of Christian traditions.[2] Their own practices of retrieval and borrowing are evidence of this wider respect for the Church catholic and its traditions, which also functions to relativize their own attachment to the denominational tradition they come from and/or belong to. They have fused the interdenominational habits of evangelicalism and the charismatic renewal with a new set of 'Deep Church' 'ancient-future' habits. This leads them to prize qualities of openness and generosity, so that they see themselves as part of a pilgrim,

---

2 As mentioned above, they are post-Vatican II Protestants.

learning Church and, not uncommonly, to describe themselves as 'post-denominational'.[3]

The ministries of women

One of the most important supplements to the Church's theology and practice in the twentieth century was without doubt the move to affirm the ministry of women in new ways. While a few smaller Christian denominations had previously affirmed the ministry of women in terms equivalent to that of men, and while women had often played remarkable and pioneering roles within the international missionary movement, it was not until the early twentieth century that mainline Protestant churches began to ordain women to the ministry of word and sacrament. What began as a trickle in the early decades, with Congregationalists among the early movers, increased exponentially from the 1950s onwards, as Presbyterians, Methodists, Baptists and most recently Anglicans moved to open ordination to both women and men (although not all provinces; England, for example, has not yet admitted women as bishops). The Roman Catholic Church and the various Orthodox churches continue to be resolutely opposed to the ordination of women as priests, although since the 1970s Roman Catholic women have been able to become Extraordinary Ministers of the Eucharist. In one sense it seems ironic to use the language of supplementing to refer to one half of the communion of saints, who have been a working, singing, thinking, praying, suffering, celebrating presence within the body of Christ since the apostolic era. However, the explicit changes in women's status and role over the past century or so have represented a crucial and a decisive 'supplement' to existing patterns of Christian practice.

---

3 In my experience this applies just as strongly to groups currently located within mainline denominations, where I have heard many people say: 'Our church is linked to the Methodist/Anglican/Presbyterian Church, but I see myself as more post-denominational.'

I noted in an earlier discussion of tradition that a move such as this, when it is born out of theological principle, relativizes the status of tradition and we might add the pre-existing *lex orandi*, since it involves the Church in confessing that until the change was made it had not previously rightly discerned and practised the will of God in this respect. This supplement was inherited by the emerging constituency, but it has been embraced by them in a thoroughgoing way. I know of no groups associated with emerging church that have supported a theological position restricting the ministry of women.[4] This move reflects both the revisionist theological thinking on the role of women within mainline Protestant denominations and the influence of Pentecostalism and the Charismatic Renewal. (Although many groups influenced by the Pentecostal/charismatic movements remain conservative on the question of women's ordination, there have been wider diffusive effects of this increased theological emphasis upon the Spirit being poured out on both women and men and equipping them with gifts for ministry.) The emerging project, wherever I have encountered it and whatever struggles it faces in practice to realize this, imagines the future of the Church as a shared partnership between women and men, rooted in a fundamental equality of status and calling.

The 'laity'[5]

Another area of supplementing has to do with the question of the identity and ministry of what is traditionally called 'the laity' in opposition to 'the clergy'. In the work done by Ryan

---

4 This is, of course, not to say that issues of patriarchy and sexism do not exist in emerging groups; they most certainly do, as in all churches.

5 On the 'ambiguities' of the term and its 'questionable reference', see Paul Lakeland's chapter on 'The Laity', in G. Mannion and L. Mudge (eds), *The Routledge Companion to the Christian Church*, London and New York: Routledge, 2008, pp. 511ff.

Bolger and Eddie Gibbs,[6] which is the closest thing we have to a survey or map of 'emerging churches', it was striking how the majority of groups they referenced were founded and led by non-ordained women and men. This represents another area in which the Church: Emerging is very much influenced by the free church, evangelical and charismatic roots of many of its founders and activists, although we can also see here the influence of 'lay' Christian communities like Iona and Taizé. Thinking back to the first move we discussed, that of 'auditing', the emphasis on lay activism and involvement is one of the low church Protestant distinctives that was valued and held to by at least the first generation of those who developed the emerging project. This was combined with a confidence about church planting and originating new groups from scratch, which also owed much to the evangelical world and its missional confidence.

A theology of the laity remains a strangely ambivalent and troublesome topic within ecumenical theology. Roman Catholic theologian Paul Lakeland notes that:

> There is a certain irony, as peculiar as it is revealing, to the fact that theology is almost bereft of sustained reflection on the history and theological significance of these 'laity', over 95 per cent of the members of the Christian church through the ages. Theologically speaking, the Christian laity have been all but invisible for most of the last fifteen hundred years.[7]

Lakeland's edgy account displays his own particular frustrations and quarrels with Roman Catholic practice, but the mainstream ecumenical instruments of the WCC have also struggled over the years to articulate a coherent theology of the laity. Recognized as a neglected theme in the early ecumenical decades, Hans-Ruedi Weber wrote in 1963 of 'The Rediscovery of the Laity in the Ecumenical Movement', but at the same

---

6 E. Gibbs and R. Bolger, *Emerging Churches*, London: SPCK/Grand Rapids, MI: Baker Academic, 2006.

7 Lakeland, 'The Laity', p. 511.

time bemoaned the continuing lack of attention shown by the Faith and Order Commission. Weber quotes from a 1961 essay, in which the Dutch Reformed ecumenist Hendrik Kraemer claimed:

> 'Never in church history, since its initial period, has the role and responsibility of the laity in Church and world been a matter of so basic, systematic, comprehensive and intensive discussion in the total oikoumene as today.' This discussion 'is a totally new phenomenon', it 'implies a new examination and general reshaping of all ecclesiologies, which we have had for centuries' and it 'is the most important aspect of the longing for the renewal of the Church which arises in the Churches all over the world'.[8]

Half a century later, however, mainstream ecumenism remains so deeply troubled and preoccupied by questions of mutual recognition of ministries that it still struggles to engage with Christian churches whose practice rejects the clerical paradigm or radically relativizes its operation. Many emerging groups were constituted and developed by a surge of creative energy and activity on the part of a group, which was not 'led' by a single ordained individual. As they have explored their own identity and ecclesiality, such groups have found themselves confused and dismayed by the negotiations between their own approach to working as 'lay' collectives and the restrictions on practice insisted on by denominations they related to. This has provoked a good deal of soul-searching, with two main outcomes. Groups have either gravitated towards independence from or alignment with existing denominational structures. Within the UK, the Fresh Expressions programme established

---

8 This quote represents Hans-Ruedi Weber's translation of a 1961 article by Kraemer in Dutch; see Stephen Neill and Hans-Ruedi Weber, *The Layman in Christian History*, London: SCM Press/Geneva: World Council of Churches, 1963, p. 391 n.1. Kraemer's major writing on this topic is found in his *The Theology of the Laity*, London: Lutterworth, 1958, reprinted by Regent College Publishing in 1998.

by the Methodist Church and the Church of England represented a move by these institutions to hug emerging groups
close and embrace the currents of renewal they represented.
Another consequence of this, however, and a condition of the
institutional recognition on offer, was that emerging groups
conformed to the polity of one of these churches. Particularly
within the Church of England, therefore, there has been a steady
pattern of lay activists, who were pioneers and leaders within
emerging groups, presenting themselves to the denomination
for ordination. A key factor driving this was the experience
of groups who were under pressure either to discontinue or to
'regularize' their celebrations of Communion (or to lose their
connection with the denomination). Many groups resolved this
at first by bringing in an ordained 'celebrant' from outside the
group, and while this worked well in some cases it did not
work for others.

In considering these two options of independency and alignment, it is helpful, I think, to reflect on the continuing poverty
of theological reflection on 'the laity' and the continuing nov-
elty of such reflection as an ecumenical theological topic. For
those like myself who are not happy to see the lay dynamics of
alt/emerging groups absorbed without remainder into existing
patterns of ordination,[9] the work of Jürgen Moltmann, Miroslav Volf and John Howard Yoder offers some important and
credible theological alternatives, from thinkers who have been
heavily involved in and committed to ecumenical dialogue.[10]

The disturbing supplement that we have been taught to call
'the laity' has reasserted itself in the emerging church conversa-

---

9 Albeit bespoke ones known as 'Pioneer' ministry, which has been introduced as an ordination track within the Church of England.

10 See Jürgen Moltmann, *The Church in the Power of the Spirit*, London: SCM Press, 1977, on the charges to the community and assignments
within the community; see Miroslav Volf, *After Our Likeness*, Grand Rapids, MI: Eerdmans, 1998 on ministry as of the *bene esse* but not the *esse* of
the Church; see John Howard Yoder, *Body Politics: Five Practices of the
Christian Community Before the Watching World*, Scottsdale, PA: Herald
Press, 2001, on 'the rule of Paul'.

tion in ways that call for further theological reflection, if it is not simply to have been a supplement suppressed.

Politics

The rediscovery of the Church as a political community has been a powerful journey of discovery for many emerging groups. I recognize that this is also an area where there are significant Christian traditions available for retrieval, but I would argue both that there has been a convergence of different sources and influences into a distinctively new moment of reception and that for the evangelical/charismatic traditions that have largely fed emerging church, this was an area where there was a pre-existing deficit.

Of the streams that fed the spirituality and liturgical repertoire of alt worship and emerging church, both the Taizé and Iona communities were marked by deep commitments to peace and reconciliation and the influence of *Sojourners*,[11] felt also through the Greenbelt festival in England, was animated by a desire to recover and deepen an evangelical witness for peace and justice. *Sojourners* introduced evangelicals to the voices of Thomas Merton and Dorothy Day and to the Catholic Worker Movement. What made *Sojourners* such a distinctive voice in the 1970s was the continuing polarization of evangelical and liberal churches, with peace and justice seen as 'liberal' preoccupations, which displaced a concern for evangelism. The work of John Stott, Rene Padilla, Orlando Costas and others, given a strategic expression in the 1974 Lausanne Covenant,[12] allowed for a new articulation of evangelical social concern. Jim Wallis' *Agenda for Biblical People* (1976) and Ron Sider's *Rich*

---

11 Intriguingly, the magazine was originally called *The Post-American*!

12 This landmark statement was written for and adopted by 2,300 evangelicals at the 1974 International Congress on World Evangelization in Lausanne, Switzerland. The text is widely available online: www.lausanne.org/covenant.

Christians in an Age of Hunger (1977) became iconic texts for a rising generation of 'radical evangelicals'. Meanwhile, John Howard Yoder's *The Politics of Jesus* (1972) had become a symbol of a resurgent Anabaptist/Mennonite influence, which would reach an ever wider audience from the 1980s, particularly through the advocacy of Stanley Hauerwas.[13] Yoder's work and the new visibility of the Anabaptist vision were particularly important for ecclesiology, because of its stress on the Church as a 'body politic', an exemplary community practising peace and justice in the rhythms of its own life.[14]

But the major global influence from the 1960s onwards was to be that of a range of post-colonial theologies, in particular Latin American liberation theology. In ecclesiology, reports of the Base Christian Communities offered a powerful vision of the Church as a prophetic community *of* the poor whose worship and Bible reading, sacramental life and prayers was born out of theological reflection on their material circumstances and God's power to transform them. In the USA, the hopes of earlier generations of African-American prophetic leaders were given a decisive public articulation by Martin Luther King in the Civil Rights movement. This fed the work of James Cone and others in shaping a black liberation theology from the 1970s, with Cone's *God of the Oppressed* a defining text.[15] In the UK, *The Social God* by Anglo-Catholic radical Kenneth Leech and evangelical Bishop David Sheppard's *Bias to the Poor* offered introductions to liberation theology, contextualized for inner-city England in the Thatcher years.[16] Walter Wink's creative development of Oscar Cullman's legacy in New Testament theology produced a wave of reflection on 'principalities and

---

13 See also Stuart Murray Williams, *The Naked Anabaptist*, Scottdale, PA: Herald Press/Milton Keynes: Paternoster, 2011.

14 John Howard Yoder, *The Politics of Jesus*, 2nd edition, Grand Rapids, MI: Eerdmans, 1994; and *Body Politics*.

15 James H. Cone, *God of the Oppressed*, Maryknoll, NY: Orbis/London: SPCK, 1975.

16 Kenneth Leech, *The Social God*, London: Sheldon Press, 1981; and David Sheppard, *Bias to the Poor*, London: Hodder, 1983.

powers' from 1984 onwards, which captured and stimulated the imagination of his readers across a wide range of churches and theological traditions.[17] In Old Testament theology, Walter Brueggemann's work was also widely read and helped to foster a new understanding of the political significance of a biblical-ecclesial imagination. From the 1980s onwards and under the influence of practice at WCC gatherings, the Iona Community led the way in introducing UK churches to a new repertoire of World Church songs – reversing the colonial direction of travel for church music.

This new convergence of themes was named ecumenically between the World Council of Churches Assemblies at Vancouver 1983 and Seoul 1990 as 'Justice, Peace and the Integrity of Creation' (JPIC). The presence of the last two initials was a testimony to the rise in importance of environmental theology – a rise given initial impetus by the advent of the atomic era in 1945 and fed from 1972 by the space programme's 'God's eye-view' pictures of a fragile 'blue marble'.[18]

As with liturgical retrieval, it was crucial that there were books, festivals, networks and organizations that mediated these politicized visions of church and discipleship to a wider public. Alt worship and emerging church inherited this new JPIC ecclesiology as a theological birthright and did so at a moment when the ground-clearing work of Stott and others within the evangelical world was already a done deal.[19] Understandings of the Church as *polis* and the Church's political witness were available and

---

17 In particular the 'powers trilogy': *Naming the Powers, Engaging the Powers*, and *Unmasking the Powers*, Philadelphia: Fortress, 1984, 1986 and 1992.

18 The 1972 Apollo mission took a photograph of Earth from space known as 'the Blue Marble', which became an iconic image, not least for the growing environmentalist movement. Francis Schaeffer, founder of L'Abri, had given an early lead among evangelicals in his theological advocacy for environmental issues.

19 Another marker of this was the creation of TEAR Fund, the evangelical relief and development charity, in 1968, with Stott as chair for almost three decades. In the USA, World Vision had been in existence since 1951 and the UK's larger ecumenical relief organization Christian Aid since 1945.

even obvious supplements to the thinly politicized ecclesiology which many low church Protestants had inherited.[20]

Missiology

From the outset, the alt/emerging conversation was strongly influenced by missiology and the concept of *missio Dei*. In his hugely influential 1991 book *Transforming Mission*,[21] the South African theologian David Bosch used paradigm theory to identify key shifts in how mission practice was conceived and inculturated from the beginnings of the Christian era. In the final section of the book, 'Elements of An Emerging Ecumenical Missionary Paradigm', Bosch traced the development of ecumenical theologies of mission in the twentieth century and gave a strong endorsement to the missional ecclesiology set out in *Lumen Gentium*, the Second Vatican Council Constitution on the Church.[22] He also emphasized the crucial role played in this ecumenical development by Karl Barth's 'magnificent and consistent missionary ecclesiology'.[23] Bosch described how the concept of *missio Dei* had enabled a shift from a mindset centred on missions as an activity of the Church to one in which God is the subject of mission and the Church is sent by God within the *missio Dei*. This shift of perspective decentred the eurocentric and colonial perspective in which Western churches were 'sending' churches and 'the mission field' was 'overseas'. In its place came a new 'emerging missionary ecclesiology' in which the Church was seen as essentially missionary, or missional. In another, less well-known work, *Believing in the Future*,[24] Bosch pointed to the need for a missiology of Western culture, echoing calls made since

---

20 By this I mean that all ecclesiologies are politicized; they have political consequences and occupy political positions, knowingly or unknowingly.

21 David Bosch, *Transforming Mission*, Maryknoll, NY: Orbis, 1991.

22 Bosch, *Transforming Mission*, p. 371.

23 Bosch, *Transforming Mission*, p. 373.

24 Valley Forge, PA: Trinity Press International, 1995.

the 1928 IMC Jerusalem conference for a new missiological engagement with secularism in the West. Bosch's call had already been anticipated by a number of thinkers: by the evangelical maverick Francis Schaeffer in the 1960s and 1970s, although his influence was limited and the lasting value of his work is disputed; by the later work of Lesslie Newbigin, particularly after his books *The Open Secret* and *The Other Side of 1984*;[25] by the Scottish missiologist Andrew Walls; and by the work of a (then) little-known English theologian in 1990, John Milbank, who produced *Theology and Social Theory*, the founding text of Radical Orthodoxy.[26] Milbank does not often use the word 'mission', but *Theology and Social Theory* was in its own way a radical missiological statement, which lacked Newbigin's ecumenical wisdom and charity but moved the philosophical/theological debate on to a new intellectual plane. Lamin Sanneh's *Translating the Message* has taken longer to assert its influence,[27] but has been increasingly cited in recent years, along with work by thinkers such as Stephen Bevans, Robert Schreiter and Vincent Donovan.[28]

It is significant that Newbigin's later missiology and Milbank's early manifesto were both produced in response to the increasing secularization of the United Kingdom in the last three decades of the twentieth century. It was no accident, but a clear sign of the times, that the Church of England should endorse a report in 2004 called *Mission Shaped Church* at a time when overall regular church attendance in England had dipped under 8 per cent of the population. In the face of extremely rapid decline since the early 1960s, the mainline

---

25 Lesslie Newbigin, *The Open Secret: A Theology of Mission*, Grand Rapids, MI: Eerdmans, 1978; and *The Other Side of 1984*, Geneva: Risk/World Council of Churches, 1983.

26 Oxford: Blackwell, 1990.

27 Maryknoll, NY: Orbis, 1989.

28 See, among other books, Stephen Bevans, *Models of Contextual Theology*, Maryknoll, NY: Orbis, 1992; Robert Schreiter, *Constructing Local Theologies*, Maryknoll, NY: Orbis, 1985; Vincent J. Donovan, *Christianity Rediscovered*, London: SCM Press, 1982.

Christian churches began to sharpen their missional focus in the 1990s.[29] In the UK high levels of interest in the alternative worship movement, in church planting and in 'emerging church' themes (Fresh Expressions in Church of England and Methodist terms) need to be understood against the backdrop of extensive secularization and ongoing overall church decline.[30] These trends were also well advanced in Australia and New Zealand, two other countries where there was early interest in alt worship and emerging church.[31] The comparative strength of the churches in North America, particularly in the USA, raises complex questions about the extent to which the emerging conversation has been following the same missiological agenda in Europe, Australia, New Zealand, the USA and Canada. For churches in the UK, the rapid rates of decline in membership and attendance raised urgent questions about how appropriately the gospel was being inculturated in the structures and habits of the mainline churches. For Protestants in general and evangelicals in particular, concerns about inculturation had historically been experienced as questions about effective 'attractional' communication and answered with flurries of modernization, as the 'means' were given the latest available technological or cultural *aggiornamento*.[32] It

---

29 On UK church decline see *Religious Trends 1–6*, Swindon: Christian Research, 2001–08; Callum Brown, *The Death of Christian Britain*, London: Routledge, 2001. The 1990s were designated as a 'Decade of Evangelism' – an initiative that inspired enthusiasm in some and disdain in others.

30 Some pockets of church growth, mainly among evangelicals/charismatic evangelicals and black majority congregations and mainly in urban areas, have bucked these trends, but they have been outweighed by the steady decline of mainline denominations (Protestant and Roman Catholic) over the UK as a whole. For statistical information see Peter Brierley's work in the *Religious Trends* series and the Church of England's own statistical returns.

31 See Mike Riddell, Mark Pierson and Cathy Kirkpatrick, *The Prodigal Project*, London: SPCK, 2000.

32 On the modernization of church music see Andrew Wilson-Dickson, *The Story of Christian Music*, Oxford: Lion, 1992, pp. 240–2; on evangelicals and 'means' see Pete Ward, *Selling Worship*, Milton Keynes: Paternoster, 2005, pp. 1ff. On the broader point, an explicit example of this would

has therefore been one of the missiological distinctives of the emerging conversation that engagement with the postmodern condition was seen to require something more than a further modernizing response.[33]

'Technological' supplements

The emerging conversation has been profoundly shaped by the technological and cultural supplements associated with the spread of personal computing, digital imaging and the rise of the internet. The links between technological/cultural change and the Reformation have been widely explored, particularly in relation to the role played by the printing press and the revolution in popular literacy rates in the early modern period. In a classic study, Walter Ong observed that the history of Protestantism had been inextricably bound up with the history of the printed book, but he also observed that the late twentieth century was witnessing the rise of a new 'secondary orality' which would have consequences for the human *sensorium* as profound as the early modern shift from primary orality to literacy that had preceded it.[34] Practical theology, homiletics in particular, had mused on the rise of the televisual age since the 1950s, usually commenting on the decline of 'rhetoric' (by which was meant oratory) and the need to adapt to the more intimate and conversational styles television was habituating people to. From the late 1980s onwards, cultural changes began to coalesce, not so much around the television set which had preoccupied cultural and theological commentators up to this point, as around the personal computer: above all, the globally networked personal computer, along with the mobile/cell

---

be the production of the Good News translation of the Bible in 1966, when it was initially marketed as *Good News for Modern Man*.

33 See Chapter 2 of Pete Ward, *Participation and Mediation*, London: SCM Press, 2008, for a discussion of missiology that illustrates this point.

34 Walter Ong, *Orality and Literacy*, London: Routledge, 1982.

phone and the digital camera.[35] Personal computers not only provided new ways to 'process words' or 'crunch numbers', they became portals into a new multi-layered oral–visual culture. Film and television and with them the inexorable growth of advertising had for decades been constructing a new cultural economy, in which oral–visual stimuli were aggressively and seductively used to provoke and manage desire and consumption. From the mid 1980s what the networked personal computer did, in alliance with digital photography and video, was to progressively transform the means of cultural production and the *circuit* of cultural production and consumption.[36] This had implications for ecclesiology in three main areas.

Content creation

The capacity of individual PCs to process words and enable desktop publishing was significant even before the internet enabled online dissemination. Liturgical texts, for example, were born in the era of what Clay Shirky calls 'filter then publish'[37] – an era when creating print materials required access to costly and cumbersome machinery and revising them involved making alterations to physical originals or creating new originals. The PC's capacities for digital cut and paste enabled a new era of experimentation and eclecticism for those who used written liturgies. This cut across the old 'leafing through the prayer book' pattern of 'we will use the collect on page 34, the Psalm on page 890 and the Eucharistic prayer on page 543'. Now, home-printed worship orders, which carried the same typographical authority as service books, could juxtapose old and new, institutionally authorized and home-made. From the early days of the alt worship movement, musicians

---

35 For one fascinating study see Clay Shirky, *Here Comes Everybody*, London: Penguin, 2008.

36 On cultural circuits, see Pete Ward's summary in Chapter 3 of *Participation and Mediation*.

37 Shirky, *Here Comes Everybody*, Chapter 4.

used the capacity of computers to sequence, sample and record music in bedrooms and basements to create new ambi-
ent and dance-oriented soundtracks for worship. From the
mid 1990s advances in affordable digital technology meant
that storing, editing and publishing photography and video
became possible with ordinary desktop computers. Only five
or six years after early alt worship services had worked with
'carousel' slide projectors to produce painstakingly assembled
35mm slide sequences, those working with projected images
in worship became able to draw on a digitized image library
that could be assembled and reassembled onscreen into an
endless number of sequences and seamlessly integrated with
text in PowerPoint presentations. As with the whole of the
creative industries and the arts world, content creation and
publishing of word, image and music were revolutionized by
the personal computer in ways that tended to disperse power
and opportunity, democratizing media and opening the door
wider to 'publish, then filter'.[38] It is significant that in *Emerging
Churches*, Gibbs and Bolger identified 'creating' and 'producing' as two key practices of the groups they studied.[39] This alt/
emerging emphasis on 'production' developed in intentional
contrast to patterns of the few 'selling worship' and the many
consuming it,[40] which had developed within evangelical/char-
ismatic circles. Alt/emergers aimed not only at updating styles
to reflect changing tastes;[41] many were also interested in the
subversive and deconstructive possibilities of 'creating discontent', subvertising/culture jamming and adbusting, both within

---

38 Shirky 2008, Chapter 4.

39 E. Gibbs and R. Bolger, *Emerging Churches*, London: SPCK/Grand
Rapids, MI: Baker Academic, 2006, pp. 44ff.

40 Echoing the title of Pete Ward's groundbreaking 2005 study – and
agreeing with him also that 'selling' and 'consuming' are normal social and
cultural processes, not intrinsically wicked distortions.

41 On the importance of 'taste' in worship see Frank Burch Brown, *Inclusive Yet Discerning*, Grand Rapids, MI: Eerdmans, 2009; and his fuller
treatment in *Good Taste, Bad Taste and Christian Taste*, Oxford: Oxford
University Press, 2003.

and beyond liturgy.[42] Another ecclesiological consequence of these technological supplements has been that a wider range of liturgical 'roles' were created. Some of these could be seen as postmodern versions of white surpliced actors holding up crosses, candles, thuribles and Bibles within high church liturgies, acting as enabling technicians for the liturgical action. In other cases, a new range of visual artists found their gifts and talents welcomed into the construction of liturgical space and liturgical action. This broke new ground for the involvement and empowering of 'lay' actors and was undoubtedly experienced as overwhelming, confusing and disempowering by many ordained, managerial and expert figures within the life and structures of the existing churches.

Making meaning

The advent of new technologies was not merely instrumental; it also introduced a new set of rhetorical and hermeneutical operations within the life of the Church. The recalibration of the human sensorium in mixed media environments evoked comparisons with pre-modern liturgical practice and drew new parallels with continuing 'high' liturgical traditions. Alt/emerging worship practice, in playing with a range of new visual media, began to explore a new economy of representation, in which words shared liturgical space with other signs and actions. This enabled new rhetorics and called for new hermeneutics. Tom Beaudoin's *Virtual Faith* is a rare and sophisticated early example of theological reflection on some of the issues raised here. [43] A fuller reflection on this dimension of ecclesial practice is beyond the scope of this book and this discussion, but I have no doubt that it is needed. Alt/emerging practitioners were experimenting with media formats that they were intensely, intuitively familiar with, but for which there were

---

42 See www.adbusters.org and also www.geezmagazine.org for examples and introductions.

43 San Francisco: Jossey Bass, 1998.

no real theological and liturgical 'roadmaps' to guide them. Theological reflection took place on the way, as groups and individuals reflected on what 'worked' and the ways in which newly juxtaposed rhetorics were understood to have been vehicles of Spirit-filled communication and encounter. This reflection was often enabled by new technologies, as websites and blogs opened new spaces for comment and debate.

Communicating and sharing content

A further ecclesial implication of these technological supplements, in particular the internet, was that they created new expressions of catholicity.[44] The internet opened up unprecedented opportunities for interpersonal and inter-ecclesial connection, both one on one through email with attachments and through shared hubs, where sometimes many thousands of individuals from widely separated global locations converged to lurk, comment, denounce, enthuse, download and link. Examples of mixed media liturgical innovation could be published to these sites and assessed, discussed and 'consumed' by an eclectic mix of virtual visitors, which mixed locals who had attended a service where the liturgy was in use with curious friends many time zones away. The links sections of the most popular websites could be seen as offering a new 'canon' of ideas and practices, creating well-worn virtual pathways and promoting geographically obscure practitioners to international awareness. The internet offered a new, anarchic conciliarity and a new, anarchic and dispersed ecumenism. Since the production and dissemination of the Gospels in the first century AD, methods and patterns of publication had been a crucial part of the Church's story. The revolution in publishing, distribution and debate occasioned by the internet represents a near global

---

44 Here I again have in mind Miroslav Volf's definition of catholicity in terms of inter-ecclesial openness and openness of the Church to the whole of creation.

phenomenon,[45] whose effects on our own lives and the economy of the Church we are still running to catch up with. Its effects are being variously felt and embraced by a wide range of churches, but it has been intrinsic to the alt/emerging conversation and to many aspects of networking and group formation[46] related to this.

Conclusion

Supplementing is a key move of the Church: Emerging. The forms this move takes within the emerging project reflect a distinctive cluster of concerns and practices, but they also illustrate a common and classic dimension of ecclesiology. The emerging *aggiornamento* amounts to a kind of manifesto for innovation within the Church which I believe is worthy of serious consideration and evaluation, even allowing for the mixed success of some of its more playful or eccentric examples. From the perspective of practical theology, paying attention to the range of supplements promoted will lead not just to a better understanding of the intentions of those who promoted them; reflection on the practices themselves will also reveal a play of implicit influences and logics that practitioners were not always aware of. Again, in this respect, the Church: Emerging is no different from the Church in any time or place. Innovation always involves the Church investing in media, forms and practices that it does not fully understand and cannot be fully in control of. Conservatism within the Church has and deserves an honoured place, but it is always in danger of becoming both deluded (through a failure to appreciate how what it seeks to preserve today is only there because of the creative supplements produced by earlier generations) and decadent, because

---

45 Albeit very unevenly weighted, which mirrors global patterns of wealth distribution.

46 On group formation, see Shirky, *Here Comes Everybody*, p. 31.

of its parasitic willingness to trade on the boldness of the past, while refusing to welcome or admit what is new in the present. The work of supplementing, therefore, also deserves a place of honour within the life of the Church. It is not the enemy of tradition, but an essential part of tradition.

5

'Bringing It All Back Home'
Remixing

The final move I am proposing in the hermeneutical and ecclesial spiral known as 'emerging church' is *remixing*. The metaphor is recent and musical, rooted in the musical practices of
late 1960s and early 1970s Jamaica and given new impetus
within dance music from the 1980s onwards, with the advent
of digital recording techniques. A remix allowed the combination of disparate elements into a new whole and was usually
built around a core track or melody which was recontextual-
ized and reinterpreted by allying it with a range of borrowed
and/or newly composed elements, such as a new rhythm track,
a new bassline, a rap or 'sample' of another song or a fragment
from a film or documentary soundtrack.

Analogous practices can be seen within postmodern architecture[1] and the metaphor also overlaps with ideas of *brico-
lage* in post-structuralist theory and *hybridity* in post-colonial
theory. Theologically, it can be associated with the grammar of
renewal and, from my own tradition, of reform.

Remixing both formally completes one hermeneutical spiral
and propels another one into being, as practical theology reflects again (*semper reformanda*) on how the new constellation
of ideas and practices should itself be audited.

In an essay of 1994 on 'Tradition as a Liturgical Act', Geoffrey
Wainwright draws on John Henry Newman's 1845 *Essay on
the Development of Christian Doctrine* to remark that one of
the notes of a vital tradition is, in Newman's phrase, its 'power

---

1 Charles Jencks, *The Language of Post-Modern Architecture*, Rizzoli,
NY: Wiley, 1977.

of assimilation'. Wainwright goes on to speak of 'the Church understood as an assimilative tradition'.[2] Wainwright's ecumenical ecclesiology here offers a powerful way of framing the emerging church project and of helping to do what I have tried to do throughout this book, which is to insert the conversation about emerging church into a longer church historical perspective. The Church understood as an assimilative tradition is inevitably a hermeneutical vision of the Church, one that stresses the role of the Spirit in making and remaking a Church that is always pilgrim, always a community of disciples, always learning how to be the Church – always remixing.

Wainwright's perspective also helps to thicken a further identifying claim I want to make about 'emerging church' and perhaps the closest I finally want to venture to a definition. The Emerging Church can perhaps best be understood (and defended) as an irreverent[3] new wave of grassroots ecumenism, propelled from within low church Protestantism by a mix of longing, curiosity and discontent. It is what we in the UK might call DIY[4] ecumenism, constructed by means of a series of unauthorized remixings and emboldened by an (evangelical) ecclesial culture of innovation and experimentation.[5] It is a variant of ecumenism which for the most part is ignorant of the history and protocols of institutional ecumenism, but which 'frankly might not give a damn' for them in any case, since it still carries a genetic confidence about remaking the

---

2 Geoffrey Wainwright, *Worship With One Accord: Where Liturgy and Ecumenism Embrace*, New York: Oxford University Press, 1997, p. 269.

3 I mean this, of course, institutionally and in terms of protocols, not in terms of any lack of giving glory and honour to God.

4 DIY stands for 'do it yourself' and is a standard term in the UK for amateurs undertaking home maintenance and construction by themselves.

5 Some people use the term 'entrepreneur' in this connection, but as someone whose formative years coincided with the Thatcher era I continue to loathe the high-handedness and individualism that still clings to it in my mind.

Church and its mission in response to the Spirit's prompting. Even the language of ecumenism will sound unfamiliar and irrelevant to many of those active within the emerging church conversation, since they were, for the most part, not formed in contexts that used or valued it. My decision to embrace it here as a key identifier may therefore seem strange, but I am increasingly convinced that it may be a fruitful approach, both in terms of seeking to deepen the reflection of those within the conversation as to what we are about and as a way of translating and defending 'emerging church' to at least some of its detractors.

Remixing across the spectrum

As a move within the construction of the 'emerging church', the project of remixing helps us to understand this construction in terms of a spectrum or, perhaps better, a matrix of possible outcomes, which reflect the range of ways in which emerging groups have performed the previous four moves. The kind of audit engaged in, the type of retrieval undertaken, the nature of the unbundling and the range and character of the supplements embraced will all have a decisive influence on the shape of the final remixed ecclesiology. This means that emerging church needs to be understood as a set of possibilities, which will be performed in very different ways in different locations.

In this chapter I want to explore a number of the key dynamics and judgements that animate and produce the sometimes radically different performances of remixing that have developed out of the emerging conversation.

Survival and mission

Two key dynamics, which are not mutually exclusive but are often unequally weighted and can pull groups in radically different directions, are the sensed imperatives of *survival* and of *mission*. Returning to my claim that 'emerging church' is overwhelmingly the creation of low church Protestants, with an evangelical/charismatic pedigree, the form it has taken in many places has been bound up with a generational process of relocation within, or exiting from, the church contexts and cultures in which its constituents were formed. This is what I mean by survival, and the survival in question is the faith, discipleship and ecclesial connection of those on the emerging journey. At the least, these survivors[6] have sought out new and often marginal spaces within the traditions that formed them, while many have felt the need to move outside and into a space beyond the institutional and cultural locations they came from. This journey has been understood as a form of 'exodus' or escape from a dysfunctional ecclesial space, which had been experienced variously but negatively as a place of confinement, prejudice, ignorance or banality. What people were escaping from (the negative audit) has been a powerful determinant of what they have moved towards, as also of what they have kept and carried with them on the journey. For the survivors, the imperative has typically been understood in terms of 'freedom', both from an old and for a new culture of Christian/spiritual experience and practice. In its most extreme form, this has led people to create, or carried them into, environments that were no longer to be defined as 'churches', and in this sense has arguably carried them beyond even 'emerging church'. Perhaps the best known and most widely discussed[7] example of this would be the Ikon collective in Belfast, which has embraced and pursued a radically deconstructive manifesto, resistant to any fixed label, even the label of church (although insofar as I understand their journey, I would expect them also to contest

---

6 I mean no connection here with the UK-based church family Soul Survivor, which I do not think of as being an example of emerging church.

7 Founder member Pete Rollins' writing has been widely read and discussed in the UK and North America.

and problematize the judgement of those who said they were 'not church').[8] Other groups would not relish or exhibit the theoretical 'chops' which Ikon has deployed over the years, but would also understand and identify themselves as having moved into a space that they did not wish to describe as 'church'. Groups positioned at this point of(f) the emerging matrix may still have a profound interest in retrieval, although this will often tend towards the *mystical* or *apophatic* dimensions of Christian tradition and to the work and example of figures identified by 'orthodoxy' as 'heretical'.

There are other, more muted variations on the survivor theme, which exhibit a defiant and even indignant insistence that in fact they are 'just as much church' as any ancient or recent institutional forms that claim the name. What they would have in common with their more hard-core cousins would be the desire to explore and practise their faith free from pressure and institutional authority. For this corner of the matrix, the freedom to think, to question, to doubt and to explore are crucial to their continuing participation in the Christian conversation. For this reason they tend to sit very lightly to any conventional ideas of mission or evangelism[9] and have something of a horror of attempts to 'persuade' or 'recruit' others.

---

8 The Ikon Wiki site described Ikon as: 'Inhabiting a space on the outer edges of religious life, we are a Belfast-based collective who offer anarchic experiments in transformance art. Challenging the distinction between theist and atheist, faith and no faith our main gathering employs a cocktail of live music, visual imagery, soundscapes, theatre, ritual and reflection in an attempt to open up the possibility of a theodramatic event.' http://wiki.ikon. org.uk/wiki/index.php/Main_Page (accessed 2 June 2009: the access date is important because the designation could have been changed moments after I viewed it).

9 Ikon's evangelism group famously is described as the members seeking to be evangelized by others. A cute reversal, although one that I have found grows less interesting with repetition, as they tend to over-apply the trope of reversing binary oppositions . . .

Missional

In the 'blue corner' of the matrix, we find a radically different dynamic in operation. Here we find those actors and groups who are passionate about mission and in particular about reaching unchurched and dechurched groups within society. Again the nature of their audit of the tradition is significant and needs to be analysed carefully if its subtleties are to be properly understood. A concern for mission and evangelism is already to the fore in many of the low church evangelical and charismatic settings that have been the primary feeds into the emerging church conversation. The history of modern evangelicalism since the eighteenth century has been marked by a restless concern that the 'means'[10] of evangelism and mission should be relevant and able to key into contemporary cultural forms. In respect of means, evangelicals have been the modernizers *par excellence*, even as they have understood their theological position to be 'conservative' and resistant to 'modern theology'. In the UK context, as church membership and attendance entered a sharp and apparently relentless decline from the 1960s onwards, evangelical congregations have made up the vast majority of the minority of growing churches. The relative 'success' of their missional stance has meant that most of these congregations have continued their pattern of modernizing the means to maintain relevance, with many of them investing in the models of 'praise and worship' developed within the charismatic renewal, while refining them according to the latest technological means. These congregations, I suggest, do not fit within the emerging matrix. From the late 1980s onwards, however, a number of existing and new congregations within this sector developed an internal audit or critique of this approach, which was a key factor in developing that new matrix. This reflected concerns I have already highlighted in previous chapters. A key concern was whether a developing cultural/

---

10 See here Pete Ward's discussion of David Bebbington's work in *Selling Worship*, Milton Keynes: Paternoster, 2005, pp. 13ff.

philosophical critique of modernity was calling into question the classic evangelical strategy of modernizing the means and pursuing 'relevance'. Allied to this was an internal critique of the modernized means themselves and of the cultural and aesthetic fruits of evangelical and charismatic modernization – reflected, for example, in the designations *post-charismatic* and *post-evangelical*. A further concern was whether the post-Lausanne reconciliation between evangelism and social concern and the rising challenge of a politicized, 'liberation' ecclesiology had been adequately integrated into the spirituality and practice of congregations and into their missional understanding.

It is the groups that were marked by these concerns that have been most interested and involved in creating and extending the emerging church conversation. Their critique of modernizing led them to develop a renewed interest in tradition. This and their dissatisfaction with the cultural aesthetic forms of evangelical-charismatic worship led them to explore possible retrievals of a broad range of 'catholic' spiritual practices. That critique and dissatisfaction also fuelled a more radical engagement with new technological 'means', which saw them not just exploring these instrumentally as 'jazzier' ways of putting the message across (the classic evangelical mode of engagement), but also interrogating the cultural shifts within which these new means were embedded and reflecting on the new creative and hermeneutical possibilities (and dangers) that were emerging in, with and under them. The crucial factor about these groups, however, has been that they have carried with them on this journey a deep sense of missional understanding and commitment and a belief that the remixing they were involved in was animated by and in the service of the *missio Dei*. The journey of a leading English activist and international networker such as Jonny Baker can be seen as a key example of this, as could the work of another well-known emerging blogger, 'tall-skinnykiwi', aka Andrew Jones. It is significant that Baker's institutional work location is now within a mainstream mission agency, the Anglican Church Mission Society (CMS). They represent an area of the matrix that has been involved in and responsive to the whole ambit of emerging concerns, but has continued to reflect a strongly missional dynamic and to be unembarrassed about a desire to see people come to faith and to see church communities grow. This journey has also been about survival with integrity in the face of a strong sense of unease and lack of fit with their churches of origin, but it has held to a path on which the language of 'mission-shaped Church' has continued to be prized and deployed.

Apostolicity, catholicity and the marks of the Church

Mapping the emerging matrix of remixing the Church means also taking into account a further set of dynamics to do with how we understand the nature of the Church. Here we are faced with the diversity of responses to the questions of unbundling we considered in Chapter 3. The positions taken in relation to these questions are again determinative for the various mixes possible within the emerging church. The possibilities here map on to a classic set of ecumenical questions about the nature of ecclesiality and the marks of the Church. What is at stake is how to parse the Nicene definition of the Church as one, holy, catholic and apostolic. In exploring this question we need to remember the complex mix of ecclesial traditions that have been maintained within the field of evangelical Protestantism and which have remained available to those within the emerging conversation. In particular, the ecclesial mix of the Anglican Communion has offered a powerful *via media*, which has exerted a strong gravitational pull. In the UK we should note the importance of the Church of England's *Mission Shaped Church* (2004) and the Fresh Expressions programme which flowed from it as key indicators of the potential hospitality of Anglican ecclesiology to the concerns of those engaged by the agenda of emerging church. Even before this, although it proved a messy and turbulent beginning, the willingness of the Church of England to engage with the key alt worship/alt ecclesial experiment of the Nine O'Clock Service and to move swiftly to ordain some of its key leaders in the 1990s was an early sign that this denomination was able to produce a flexible assimilative response.

We are back, therefore, in the territory marked out by Miroslav Volf in *After Our Likeness*: that is, in the midst of ecumenical debates about how to define ecclesiality and how to identify any given group as a church. Groups within the Church of England, the Church in Wales, the Scottish Episcopal Church, the Episcopal Church in the USA, the Anglican Churches of Australia, Canada and New Zealand which became part of the emerging conversation have therefore been faced with questions and choices about their polity on a local level and their connection and integration with the larger polity of the denominations/communion they are tied to. There have been carrots and sticks involved in negotiating their responses. Carrot-wise, the denominations have offered access to resources, training and support. The sticks involved have included a reduced access to such opportunities, along with, in some cases, the withdrawal of permission to use denominational buildings unless patterns of 'order' were brought in line with denominational standards.

Unsurprisingly, the most sensitive issues have been those around eucharistic presidency. The direction of travel of such groups has been towards a 'clericalizing' of their structures, with a significant number of lay leaders moving onto an ordination track. The Church of England in particular has shown some flexibility in enabling this pattern of assimilation to its tradition, by creating ordination pathways under the rubric of 'Pioneer Ministry'[11] and a legal instrument for recognizing new church plants alongside or across existing parochial boundaries, known as a Bishop's Mission Order. The upside to such flexibility is the demonstration that Anglican ecclesiology can

---

11 In 2006 the House of Bishops approved new guidelines to encourage vocations to Pioneer Ministry as a recognized focus of ordained ministry.

be hospitable to emerging church initiatives and to a broader range of 'missional' initiatives, which might not see themselves as mapping onto the emerging matrix. If there is a downside, it might be the question as to whether such a pattern of assimilation, in which the denomination 'hugs close' its potentially prodigal children, effectively neutralizes key dimensions of the emerging church challenge.

My concern here is not to pronounce a verdict on these processes but to draw attention to their significance in terms of the ways in which remixing is performed in different locations. For all the real creativity, flexibility and hospitality involved, the assimilation at work is a highly conservative one, which reinforces an episcopally ordered clericalism. The danger here is that this kind of assimilation inevitably implies a continuing judgement against other ways of recognizing ecclesiality and lawful ordination. In Volf's terms, it may continue to insist, or at least imply, that episcopal ordination is of the *esse* of the Church and not only bound up with its *bene esse*.[12] This principle is somewhat blurred in practice within the Church of England, by virtue of a degree of discretion allowed in respect of when and how someone such as myself, who is ordained within the Church of Scotland, may be allowed to take on 'clerical' roles within Anglican worship. In these contexts, emerging debates about remixing church can therefore be seen to have moved firmly into the gravitational field of older ecumenical negotiations about ecclesiality. The degree to which groups and individuals move with this assimilative gravity will shape the kind of remixing they perform and will position them on the emerging matrix.

It is, however, important to be clear that there are a number of other contexts in which this gravitational pull is not felt or not recognized. The situation is clearly different for groups that have been shaped by other traditions of ecclesiology, and have

---

12 Miroslav Volf, *After Our Likeness*, Grand Rapids, MI: Eerdmans, 1998, p. 248.

no aspiration or desire to be recognized by episcopal denominations. Some of them will, of course, experience the gravitational pull of, for example, Presbyterianism or Methodism and find themselves negotiating with the patterns of polity and the understanding of the marks of the Church (*notae ecclesiae*) operative within these and other denominational families. Others will knowingly or unknowingly move into a political space associated with various kinds of congregationalism and independency, what Volf identifies as the space of the Free Churches. This may involve them in following distinctive trajectories in relation to questions of authority, polity, ordination and presidency. Some of these may have their own internal complexity, which is itself long-standing – such as the approaches to ordination, ministry and 'presidency' within Congregationalist, Mennonite/Anabaptist and Pentecostal traditions. Some groups may draw on the work of theologians such as Moltmann and Volf to construct a new rationale for their practice within essentially independent polities, which may eschew clerical categories and individualized ordination practices altogether, while still seeking to articulate the theological basis for their practice in ways that are fully engaged with ecumenical debates and processes. This would see such groups located in a different area of the emerging matrix, but might also see them demonstrating a different and novel relationship to the ecumenical debates around assimilation. They might, for example, as we have noted before, assimilate a range of liturgical and spiritual practices without being assimilated structurally or 'politically' to the traditions that have developed or promoted these practices; or they might organize locally around the kind of High Church Mennonite identity that Stanley Hauerwas mobilizes for his literary and theological practices.

Already, then, it is becoming clear from examining these first two paired dynamics that the emerging matrix is a 'broad church' and that possibilities for remixing are multiplying. To complicate matters further, though I intend it to be a helpful complication, I want to suggest a final set of dynamics operative within the emerging church conversation.

Liberal/revisionist and conservative/orthodox

I have some hesitations about both naming and writing this section, because I realize that for some friends and fellow pilgrims I will appear to be falling back into and reinforcing categories and distinctions that they understand emerging church to be in the process of overcoming, deconstructing and consigning to history. All I can say is that I find it still to be a necessary relapse if the debates around emerging church are to be better understood and if some of the broadsides against emerging church are to be resisted. The point is a simple one, although it has to do with difference and complexity. It is that there is considerable internal theological diversity in respect of the positions espoused by groups and individuals who would locate themselves within the emerging church conversation. If the majority of those who have instigated and developed the emerging church project were formed by the traditions of a broadly evangelical theology, their journeys within this have led them to a range of theological positions and stances.[13] Some – I suggest they are a minority – have embraced a radically deconstructive route, aligning themselves with the theological and a/theological positions of thinkers such as John Caputo or Mark C. Taylor. Some have been greatly influenced by the 'deep ecumenism' of John Hick or Matthew Fox. Some, I believe a larger percentage, have taken a post-liberal or post-evangelical route,[14] identifying themselves with the work of George Lindbeck, Hans Frei, Walter Brueggemann, Miroslav Volf, Stanley Hauerwas and, perhaps, Karl Barth. Some identify

---

13 If I map these in terms of a range of recognized positions within 'academic theological debates', I am aware that they have evolved by different routes: some in direct dialogue with academic theology and some in a more instinctive and popular way, with little knowledge or awareness of academic debates. I am also aware of the limitations of 'labels'.

14 The two terms are asymmetrical – post-evangelical is a much less frequently used and less well-defined term, but it does have some purchase within this discussion.

more explicitly with parts of the programme of Radical Orthodoxy and figures such as John Milbank, Graham Ward and
Catherine Pickstock, as well as less easily categorizable figures
such as Rowan Williams, Sarah Coakley and David Ford. Some
are strongly influenced by the Anabaptist tradition, in particular the work of John Howard Yoder and James McClendon,
and the UK-based Baptist writer, Stuart Murray Williams.
Some relate positively to the contemporary Reformed and
Calvinist tradition, as developed by thinkers such as Nicholas
Wolterstorff, David Fergusson and Bruce McCormack. Some,
and again I would reckon them a major grouping within those
identified with emerging church, continue to identify strongly
as 'evangelicals' or 'radical evangelicals' and work within
the broad tradition of evangelicalism exemplified by figures such as John Stott, Stanley Grenz, Alister McGrath and
N. T. Wright, as well as, for example, Jim Wallis and Ronald
Sider.

I need to break off from this painful and unwieldy exercise
before it finally falls into absurdity. Labelling is often a mug's
game and there are so many overlaps between the categories
above, not to mention the cross-cutting influences of Eastern
Orthodoxy, liberationist theologians, missiologists and feminist
theologians, that the exercise is doomed to unravel. My thin
justification for attempting it at all is as an exercise in rebut-
tal against those who want to reduce their theological critique
of emerging church to a series of heresy hunts against figures
such as Brian McLaren, Pete Rollins, Steve Chalke and Tony
Jones. At the risk of dignifying these critics' lack of awareness
of the phenomenon they are targeting, my experience over two
decades of involvement in alt worship and emerging church
networks, blogs and conferences is that there is very significant
theological diversity within the emerging church conversation.
If critics, particularly academic critics, care at all about schol-
arly integrity and fairness, they need to take the trouble to become considerably more 'conversant' with the emerging church
than many of them have to date. If they do, they will find not
a narrow band of pluralists, deconstructors and heretics, but a

broad constellation of theological thinking and a widespread enthusiasm for theological literacy.

This broad constellation contains its fair share of theological positions, which we can roughly but reasonably map into the contrasting dynamics of 'liberal' and 'evangelical/orthodox/post-liberal' – and so produces a further set of options for the 'emerging matrix'. As someone working within practical theology, I hope I recognize when I have tried to lead an argument over rough ground and have offered readers something of a bumpy ride. To extend the metaphor, taking photographs from a vehicle moving on such a route can mean trouble focusing and lead to blurry images. To produce a set of sharper images would involve slowing down, stopping more and designing a much larger and more intensive, survey-based methodology which would test the judgements and observations I have offered here. I recognize the limitations of the analysis both in this chapter and throughout the book, but my intention has been to offer a reflection faithful to my own view of what I see of the emerging church conversation and of practice associated with it. Where I have not been able to do enough to convince readers of the scope or adequacy of my own vision of the subject, I hope I may have done enough to encourage others to move beyond my analysis and to problematize the superficial judgements of some critics.

Emerging Matrix

Ethos:	Mission		Survival
Polity:	Succession		Procession
Theology:	'Orthodox'		'Liberal'

Source, spiral matrix

A key concern of this book has been an attempt to sketch out a conceptual map of what might be going on when we speak about 'emerging church'. I began by suggesting that there are four key sources for the Church: Emerging – evangelicalism, the Charismatic Renewal, the Liturgical Movement and the Ecumenical Movement. I then used the two heuristic devices of a spiral and a matrix to unpack the term into a series of 'moves' and a field of 'dynamics', which help to both clarify and extend our understanding of what we are dealing with.

In this final section I want to shift from the more analytic tone of the discussion so far and to move towards advocacy, setting out a vision for ecclesiology in the twenty-first century, which is inspired by the action and reflection of groups involved in the emerging conversation. This seems to me to be a necessary moment within practical theology, in which we try to form some provisional judgements about what 'good practice' looks like and to take the risk of advocating how it should be developed. For those of us working within the academy and those taking part in broader debates within the Church, the risk involved is that of making ourselves vulnerable to criticism, which may both dent our reputations and hurt our feelings. None of us is immune to that kind of wounding and the language of 'worship wars' and 'culture wars' bears witness to the violence with which the Church's feuds can be pursued. What encourages hopeful risk-taking is the conviction that the collegiality of the academy and the catholic community of the Church both stand under a calling from God to be accountable for speaking the truth in love. If our work as members of these bodies is offered in love and with a sense of faith in the providence of God, then we can move forward with a sense of gratitude for those other voices in the conversation that will challenge and correct our own voices. Even when those voices are at their shrillest, the last word will always belong to the Christ who brings grace and peace, who loves the Church and gives himself for it.

Born-again ecumenism

I still find it surprising, to a degree, that my own journey has led me so clearly towards the language of ecumenism. Raised and formed in circles that were either hostile or indifferent to the ecumenical project, I only became a 'born-again ecumenist' when I began to read more deeply into the church history of the first half of the twentieth century. What I had previously downplayed as a rather eccentric, bureaucratic and liberal pre-occupation, likely to divert brave new evangelicals like myself from the real priorities of Christian activism, began to show itself as a vision of the Church far more profound than my own. I started to 'get' ecumenism for the first time. I began to see how ecumenism within Europe was a radical, contextual movement animated twice over by a deep sense of penitence in relation to 'Christian' Europe's experience of two world wars within a generation. I learned from the work of Karl Barth and Lesslie Newbigin, among others, of the deep connections between mission and ecumenism and was convicted by their sense of the scandal of Christian disunity, the obstacles it posed to effective evangelism and the painful, even gruesome way the tides of colonialism had exported the denominational divisions of Christian Europe to Southern contexts. I saw, too, how the longings for the cultural and aesthetic transformation of Christian worship within my own evangelical and Reformed experience had been felt and acted on by earlier generations of Protestant Christians, who were provoked by encounter with other traditions to an audit of their own liturgical practice and a delight in the richness of catholic tradition.

For me, these realizations came along with my attempts to reflect on experience of 'alternative worship' practice within the UK and my involvement in international internet-based conversations about alternative worship and emerging church. The two have grown together over two decades, with this book part of an ongoing journey to trace and understand the connections between ecumenism and 'emergence'. A more recent marker on this journey was the experience of reading *With the Grain of the Universe*, Stanley Hauerwas' 2001 Gifford Lectures, delivered at the University of St Andrews in Scotland.[15] Hauerwas' summoning of three witnesses from the three divided streams of Western Christianity – Roman Catholicism, the Reformed tradition and the Radical Reformation – struck a deep chord with me, as did the significance of this trialogue being given its initial[16] staging within Scotland.

Practising emerging church

There are a series of implications for ecclesial practice, for Church Pragmatics, which I draw from the analysis and argument of this book. What commends most of them, I hope, is precisely their lack of originality and their desire to be attentive and faithful to the word of scripture and the witness of the Spirit, in line with the best practice of the Church down through the centuries. What kind of Church are we learning to be?

A pilgrim Church of disciples

To return to a theme sounded at the beginning, the ecclesiology of Emerging Church is a hermeneutical ecclesiology, which understands the Church as pilgrim through history, always seeking to hasten slowly at the prompting of the Holy Spirit and to walk in the way of Jesus Christ. It is a grand vision of the Church catholic learning obedience in history as well as the local vision Newbigin speaks of in which 'the congregation is the hermeneutic

---

15 Grand Rapids, MI: Baker/London: SPCK, 2001.

16 Initial in a formal sense, since these witnesses have been constant presences threaded through Hauerwas' work over a longer period, prior to the Giffords in St Andrews.

of the gospel'.[17] It is a vision of the Church of God within the mission of God, in which the mission of God is continually trans-forming the Church, as it learns to live its own catholicity across space and time. In the twenty-first century, this carries particular implications for the churches of the North and the West as they are disciplined by the Spirit to a new attentiveness to the voices of the churches of the South and the East.

I have deliberately avoided making reference to the work of Brian McLaren so far, not as a sign of lack of esteem, but as a rejection of the way some critics virtually equate 'emerging church' with McLaren's work. Here I want to celebrate two key themes in Brian's work: his understanding of the need for humility and generosity in Christian practice. These are Christian virtues that all churches and commentators need to be formed in and they should echo daily and weekly in the confessions and intercessions of the Church's liturgy. For myself, as a believer making my home within the Reformed tradition, this vision of the Church 'always to be reformed' has a deep resonance and signals for me, a real convergence between the grammar of emergence and the grammar of reform. Where groups identifying with 'emerging church' have appeared ar-rogant or disdainful of 'inherited' or 'traditional' church and brash in their confidence about 'fresh expressions' or 'church plants', that is a cause for regret and repentance. Equally, the self-satisfied dismissal of emerging church as mere fad or ado-lescent experimentation does not do justice to the discipleship of those involved or to the gifts they may bring to other, more established locations of Christian practice.

A richly storied, richly memoried Church

It is, I believe, one of the great strengths of the emerging church conversation that it has shaken off the amnesiac tendencies of

---

17 See Lesslie Newbigin, *The Gospel in a Pluralist Society*, London: SPCK, 1989, Chapter 18.

modernist evangelicalism and has worked to refresh the church historical memory of low church Protestants. Alister McGrath quotes early Anabaptist Sebastian Franck's extreme sixteenth-century verdict that 'for 1400 years now there has existed no gathered Church nor any sacrament'.[18] It is possible that at times the desire of some within the emerging church may have swung to the opposite extreme, perhaps even taking Radical Orthodoxy as a sophisticated provocation and justification for doing so. Thankfully, the alternatives do not reduce to presumptious primitivism or to overcooked (eurocentric) medievalism. The past does not have to be venerated, but the communion of saints has to be received as a key dimension of ecclesiology and indeed of Christian experience. This certainly includes, but it also goes beyond, the helpful formulations of ancient-future[19] or 'Deep' church[20] towards an understanding of the whole sweep of church history as a graced and dangerous inheritance, which needs to be received critically under the guidance of the Holy Spirit. An overemphasis on 'patristic' traditions may fail to leave room for the fresh theological illumination that comes through, for example, Anabaptist or feminist theology and exposes the shadow side of otherwise rich and exemplary early or medieval constellations of belief and practice. The reading of church history is itself a theological practice that is always in need of sanctification, and post-colonial theology and missiology offer crucial prophetic resources for this work.[21] The aspiration of those aligned with emerging church to understand themselves as part of a richly storied, richly memoried Church is something they have learned from the modern and post-modern ecumenical conversation and it is a promising move

---

18 Alister McGrath, *Christian Theology: An Introduction*, Oxford: Blackwell, 1994, p. 415.

19 Robert Webber, *Ancient-Future Faith*, Grand Rapids, MI: Baker Academic, 1999.

20 C. S. Lewis' phrase, adopted by Andrew Walker and Luke Bretherton in their collection *Remembering the Future*, Milton Keynes: Paternoster, 2007.

21 Which is both our work and the work of God at work in us.

within their discipleship. It is also an aspiration that needs to be worked at across many levels of the Church's practice, from support for academic scholarship to accessible catechism and appropriate liturgical expression in local congregations.

A Church apostolic and catholic

In my experience, evangelical churches tend to be hyper-conscious of stressing the Church's apostolicity and holiness, but more reserved in their attentions to its unity and catholicity. If the emerging church conversation has rebalanced that, I believe it will have done well. If, however, it becomes inarticulate in terms of confessing the Church's apostolicity, it will create a new and dangerous imbalance. Here I confess my own continuing evangelical and Reformed credentials in terms of my conviction that a commitment to the unique status and authority of the biblical witness within the life of the Church is not only wholly compatible with the emerging church project, but essential to the well-being of any Christian Church. As the *Westminster Confession* says, 'it is to be believed, obeyed . . . and received, because it is the Word of God'.[22] While I recognize and respect the opinions of those who variously hold to a belief in the crucial role of the (male?) episcopate in the 'apostolic succession',[23] I stand with Moltmann's more inclusive understanding of 'apostolic procession', which I understand primarily in terms of ongoing faithfulness to the apostolic proclamation. In Volf's terms, I hold ordination to be a matter of the *bene esse* and not of the *esse* of the Church. I therefore believe firmly that a local church can be recognized as properly apostolic, by virtue of its confession and practice, without reference to any episcopal authority. Despite a growing love for and respect for the Roman Catholic Church, I remain stubbornly unconvinced of the need to be found within what John

22 *Westminster Confession*, Ch. 1. para. 4.
23 See Volf, *After Our Likeness* for a helpful comparative discussion of Orthodox and Roman views.

Milbank, with typical (and it has to be said very optimistic) presumption, describes as the 'potential Conciliar authority of the Rome–Constantinople–Canterbury triangle'.[24]

My point here is not that my view carries much, if any, weight in this broader conversation, it is rather that the shape of our ecclesiology on this point is crucial in relation to the ecclesial status of many groups who identify with the emerging church. The claim I want to associate myself with is that to the extent such congregations bear a faithful witness to the gospel in word, baptism, Eucharist and ethics, they are part of the Church apostolic. I also want to agree with Volf here in asserting that such recognition of other churches is itself a performance of the Church's catholicity. The implications of this position are that I, while making my home within a Presbyterian church, also recognize the ecclesiality of the independent, 'Congregationalist' Urban Expressions church plant two miles away in Possilpark, one of Glasgow's poorest urban areas; and that I recognize the ecclesiality of a Mennonite congregation in the Democratic Republic of Congo, of a new monastic community in a downtown area of Philadelphia, USA and of a Pentecostal congregation in Mexico City. I accept and affirm their ecclesiality in the same terms as I accept and affirm the ecclesiality of my own local Church of Scotland in the West End of Glasgow parish and of the local Roman Catholic parish in Maryhill. Of each of them I would want to say what the World Council of Churches Porto Alegre statement says: 'Each Church is the Church catholic and not simply a part of it. Each church is the Church catholic, but not the whole of it.'[25]

---

24 Milbank in John Milbank and Simon Oliver (eds), *The Radical Orthodoxy Reader*, London: Routledge, 2009, p. 396. Optimistic, of course, because Rome does not (yet?) recognize Canterbury's version of 'apostolic succession'. So Milbank is turning the rest of us mere Protestants away from a train he does not (yet?) have a ticket for himself!

25 World Council of Churches, Porto Alegre Document PRC 01.1 Rev. www.oikoumene.org/resources/documents/wcc-commissions/faith-and-order-commission/i-unity-the-church-and-its-mission/called-to-be-the-one-church-the-porto-alegre-ecclesiology-text.html.

I am aware that my theological convictions about the nature of the Church make this an easy and, more than that, a joyful thing for me to affirm, while for others their inability to affirm this may be a source of great pain and sadness. I also accept that their motives are overwhelmingly not based on arrogance or exclusivity[26] but on a desire to be faithful to Christ, and hope they may accept that views such as mine are not merely motivated by a facile desire to be 'inclusive'.

I recognize, as I said above, that many groups who are part of the emerging conversation may feel themselves drawn in faithfulness to the gravitational pull of an episcopal communion. Some will make this journey while reserving their willingness to fully affirm the ecclesiality of non-episcopal congregations and to share in the Eucharist with them. Others may not feel able to do this. It is important, I believe, to recognize that these journeys within and 'through' emerging church are already under way in many places and will begin in many others. This may well be a painful thing for those who have felt themselves to be on a shared path and find it diverges at this point. Here, too, it may be that the ecumenical movement, with its history of seeking to stay together in the face of continuing painful differences of understanding, may offer a resource of story and practice to its younger 'emerging' cousins.

A liturgically versatile Church

Questions of worship and liturgical practice have never been far from this discussion and they occupy a key place in my vision of future practice. My vision is of a Church that can embrace a new capacity for liturgical versatility, without falling over into incoherence or dilettantism. Perhaps ironically, some of my preferred role models here could be Church of England bishops, who exercise their ministry to a very diverse

---

26 I include my Anglican brother John Milbank here, despite my rankling at his rhetoric. I rate him one of the great theologians of our age and remain attentive to and often in awe of his work.

array of Anglican styles within a single diocese. At their best, when they are not just gritting their teeth and bearing it, they exemplify a kind of pastoral versatility in relation to liturgy when they move between conservative evangelical, charismatic evangelical, liberal-catholic, conservative Anglo-Catholic congregations and find something to affirm in each. The situation is different for a congregation, but versatility can coexist with integrity.[27] The genius and the burden of worshipping congregations who identify with emerging church is their attempt to span what can be an unusually wide range of liturgical codes and styles. While this can lapse into incoherence and sometimes even into farce, I want to argue that their pilgrimage to learn new ways to worship with theological and cultural integrity should be honoured. In their auditing, retrieval, unbundling and supplementing, these congregations are genuine heirs of a radical strand within the Liturgical and Ecumenical movements as well as reformers in respect of their traditions of origin. In their sometimes fumbling, sometimes dazzling engagements with new media and technology, they are prophets and pioneers, whose work may enrich the worship and mission of the wider Church in a host of ways. So many of us within the mainstream churches manage to tolerate dullness, pomposity, self-importance, obscurantism and sentimentality in liturgical performance better than we are able to tolerate risk.

In many instances, the versatility proposed is hardly revolution. A low-key remix of Presbyterian worship, to take an example close to home, may involve a new openness to silence, a broader range of accents and actors voicing the liturgy, a more regular celebration of Communion, a greater use of ritual and symbolic action. A more radical remix of Anglican liturgy might involve a decentring of the voices and bodies of the clergy, the liturgical use of photography and video, the use of music beyond classical and soft rock genres. In neither case

---

27 Anglicans are often good examples of this congregationally, with many parish churches offering radically different styles of worship at 8 a.m., 11 a.m. and 7 p.m.

has the possibility (or necessity) of sermon or *ordo* been excluded. In both cases, the cultural and liturgical politics have been unsettled. Above all, what inspires me is a vision of worship that is versatile in its willingness to unsettle the tribalisms and fundamentalisms of 'high' and 'low' church distinctives and to think both more critically and more creatively about the ecclesial ideologies that are being carried by liturgical habits. Dominant worship styles still bear very strongly the marks of their male provenance, whether the monological authoritarianism of the preaching station, the rock star performance aura of charismatic praise or the camp paternalism of high church ritual. Each of those styles deserves to be better exposed to the glorious freedom of the Holy Spirit and to be claimed and performed more fully by women and men of post-patriarchal sensibilities.

A *mission-shaped Church*

While recognizing that parts of the emerging matrix are significantly reticent about the language of mission and evangelism, it is significant that missiological concerns have generally had a high profile within the emerging conversation. Missiology, in particular post-colonial missiology, insists that questions of culture be given a greater prominence within theological reflection and that incongruities between church practice and contemporary culture be critically examined and assessed. The characteristically Christian practice of translation and the key Reformation emphasis on vernacular practice call for an ongoing critical awareness of how the Church's practice is inculturated and of how it participates in cultural circuits of production, representation and consumption. The Church's too often uneasy relationship with the arts, veering regularly between patronage, atrophy, instrumentalism and fear, reflects a tendency to cultural entrenchment and a political stance that often coalesces defensively around the cultural politics of a dominant class. The emerging conversation has looked to missiology for

resources in facing the challenge of how to contextualize the proclamation, liturgical performance, pastoral care and deliberations
of Christian congregations within postmodern Western societies.
At its best it has worked to move beyond the instrumentalism of
evangelical practice, in which new means were too often treated
as the spoonful of cultural sugar that helped the medicine of the
gospel go down. An alternative vision of ecclesial practice here
would be one that takes seriously the cultural/aesthetic/rhetorical
mediation of the Church's mission, but sees theological reflection
on such mediation as itself a gospel task and concern.

   This calls for a more developed hermeneutical dialogue between gospel and culture. In recent decades the most prominent
model for this within practical theology, sometimes referred to
as a 'Chicago' approach, has been a reworking of Paul Tillich's
method of 'correlation' towards a 'revised, critical model of
correlation'.[28] This has subsequently been directly criticized by
James K. A. Smith, who stresses the alternative Barth/'Yale'/
Radical Orthodoxy approach in which theology is seen to offer a more thoroughgoing alternative 'narration' of the world,
which is 'more mediating, but less accommodating'.[29] My sym-
pathies lie more with Smith's proposals for the way forward,
but it is possible to overstress the oppositions involved in a
way that underplays or overstates the relative value of each
method. Both can be and have been used fruitfully in ways that
extend the Church's capacity for missional reasoning. Stephen
D. Long and Nancy Ruth Fox offer an insightful formulation
of what is at stake in their volume *Calculated Futures*:

   Theology and social analysis are always already linked.
   When we are doing theology we are already doing political

---

   28 Associated with the work of Seward Hiltner, David Tracy and Don
Browning. See Elaine Graham, Heather Walton and Frances Ward, *Theological Reflection: Methods*, London: SCM Press, 2005, Chapter 5, for a
discussion of these approaches.
   29 A phrase found on p. 2 of *Radical Orthodoxy: A New Tradition*,
London: Routledge, 1999; for Smith's discussion see his 2004 volume *Introducing Radical Orthodoxy*, Grand Rapids, MI; Baker Academic pp. 25ff.

and economic analysis. When economists are doing econom-
ics they are also doing theology. The question is which theology is being done, not if it is being done, Everything is
theological . . .

To use God for political or economic ends is to take God's
name in vain. That everything is theological then means something different from this; it means that everything which is
creature, by virtue of being creature, bears some sign, some
mark, some relation to the Creator and theologians must
narrate all those creatures within the divine economy.[30]

To be a mission-shaped Church, I believe, is to embrace this
wider project of narrative practice in respect of the whole of life
and to perform it through the Church's ministries of worship,
preaching, evangelism, pastoral care and prophetic action as
well as its theological reflection. The total missional expression
of this narrative practice involves the dispersed witness of the
body of Christ in all the various secular callings of its members.

Such a vision of the mission-shaped Church offers a necessary corrective to the overly thin accounts of gospel and culture
relations, which have been unfavourably audited by emerging
groups who have 'taken against' mission and may also offer a
way to rethink the actions of more 'survivalist' groups as themselves deeply missional. However, I also want to stand behind
the passionate concern of 'missional' groups to see people become baptized and communicant disciples of Jesus Christ and
to see churches grow. I do not share the ambivalence of some
within emerging circles over these aims and I believe that they
are vital and compelling desires within the life of the Christian
churches, which can be fully embraced, worked and prayed for
by those within the emerging church conversation. Finally, I
want to again sound an ecumenical note here, by stressing the
crucial theological connection between the Church's unity and
its witness to the gospel. If we are to be the Church our Lord

---

30 Waco, TX: Baylor University Press, 2007, pp. 6–7.

mandated in John 13.34–35 and prayed for in John 17.21, we must pray for a deep love for our brothers and sisters in Christ to be given concrete expression in our Christian practice. To the extent that the emerging conversation displays any narrow contempt for parts of Christ's body or disdains the call to seek loving communion with them, it is failing to learn to be Church.

A political-prophetic Church

The final set of implications for ecclesial practice that I want to highlight is rooted in the vision of the Church as a political community, exercising a practical prophetic witness in the world. Karl Barth (allegedly) said that to clasp our hands together in prayer marks the beginning of an uprising against the disorder of the world.[31] Stanley Hauerwas, speaking of the Church's practices of Baptism and Communion, has said that 'these are the essential rituals of our politics'.[32] The Church's political identity is rooted in its confession of the lordship of Jesus Christ, set against every idolatrous claim to authority and mastery that confronts it within human history. Many of us who came to the emerging church conversation did so from evangelical backgrounds where individualistic understandings of salvation and sanctification had deprived the gospel of its sharp political edges and its demanding political graces. We have valued the way in which such an audit has been pressed upon us by retrievals of more rounded understandings from church history, unbundlings of Constantinian habits and the challenge of subversive ecclesiological supplements rooted in the global witness of the contemporary Church. The grace of such pressure continues in our own struggle to live as the church within our own social and political contexts, given again and again as we clasp our hands in prayer, as we share

---

31 I have not been able to find the source of this widely used quotation.
32 Stanley Hauerwas, *The Peaceable Kingdom: A Primer in Christian Ethics*, London: SCM Press, 2003, p. 108.

in the political rituals of bath and meal. The theologian Reinhard Hutter has suggested that we can think about inner and
outer circles of the *notae ecclesiae*, of constitutive practices
that mark the Church publicly as the space of God's *oiko-
nomia*. The inner circle (word and sacrament) belongs to the
Church's identity across time, while the outer circle marks the
Church's faithful witness to God in particular times and places.
The Church's witness against slavery, the resistance of the
Confessing Church to Nazism, the Church's witness against
apartheid – where these took place, they marked the Church
publicly as the Church there and then. These two circles do not
compete with one another and both markings are necessary to
the Church's public life. So the Church's political identity is
discerned and performed in these contextual remixings. In a
passage I have often returned to, Richard Bauckham writes in
The Theology of the Book of Revelation:

> one of the functions of Revelation . . . is to purge and refur-
> bish the Christian imagination . . . It recognises the way a
> dominant culture, with its images and ideals, constructs the
> world for us, so that we perceive and respond to the world in
> its terms. Moreover, it unmasks this dominant construction
> of the world as an ideology of the powerful which serves to
> maintain their power. In its place, Revelation offers a different
> way of perceiving the world which leads people to resist and
> to challenge the effects of the dominant ideology. Moreover,
> since this different way of perceiving the world is fundamen-
> tally to open it to transcendence, it resists any absolutising of
> power or structures or ideals within this world. This is the
> most fundamental way in which the church is called always
> to be counter-cultural. The necessary purging and refurbish-
> ing of the Christian imagination must, of course, always be
> as contextual as Revelation was in its original context, but
> Revelation can help to inform and to inspire it.[33]

---

33 Cambridge: Cambridge University Press, 1993, p. 159.

The political witness of the Church involves, in Bauckham's memorable phrase, the 'purging and refurbishing' of the Christian imagination, by our participation in the political rituals of word and sacrament, as the triune God works in us to make us and mark us as the Church.

Conclusion

The metaphor of remixing, like the emerging church conversation as a whole, is born out of desire. This desire originated primarily within low church Protestantism, to also be the Church in ways that we did not learn within our own backgrounds and traditions.

For some this desire is answered by shifting between Christian denominations; by becoming Roman Catholic, or Orthodox or Anglican. For others it is answered by planting new expressions of Church, which are formally or institutionally 'independent'. For others it is answered by pursuing an ecumenical project of reform within the denomination we have long been part of. The possibility of individuals and groups making these very different moves is what makes mapping and understanding the emerging church conversation a complex and frustrating business. What is clear is that within this conversation, questions of the faith and order of the Church continue to be contested in various ways, so that there are no singular outcomes or answers. The existence of such a conversation bears witness to a convergence of questions, concerns and interests within a series of virtual and physical dialogical spaces, where people have found one another and engaged one another. The outcomes and effects of this conversation are many and varied, but they include thousands of attempts to remix the Church in many different local situations, across a range of countries. The value and faithfulness of these remixes will be tested in practice and variously audited by those within and around them, as well as being caught up, we may say, in the ongoing divine audit of the Church's life. That audit will also be a test of the desires they were born out of. Has it been a desire to follow Christ, the only King and Head of the Church into a larger understanding of what it means to be the one, holy, catholic and apostolic Church? Has it been a desire to respond to the promptings of the Holy Spirit, who gives birth to the Church and sustains it in its life? For now, the only answer to those questions may be a circular one and it may look like the one Anglican theologian Timothy Gorringe gives in his book *The Education of Desire*:

> The church exists, said Augsburg, where the gospel is preached (*docetur*) and the sacraments rightly administered (Art. 7). The church exists, we may say, where human desire is educated, disciplined, by Word and sacrament.[34]

---

34 London: SCM Press, 2001, p. 103.

Conclusion

I am happy to acknowledge that this is a book whose arguments surf waves generated by bigger fish than myself. Also, switching metaphors to make a slightly different point, I recognize that while the book has raised some very weighty issues in ecumenical theology, it has not attempted to do much of the heavy lifting involved in addressing the central questions of ecumenical ecclesiology. It is, rather, a book that has tried to tell a story, to propose a hermeneutical model, to trace some genealogical connections, to point out family resemblances and to make some programmatic suggestions about how and where further work might take place. I hope that in future I may be able to do something more to help in addressing some of the tough questions the emerging church conversation cannot and should not avoid.

I suggested in the Introduction that even if the term 'Emerging Church' was to die a sudden death, it might at least deserve a decent epilogue, or even an epitaph. There has been a fair amount of 'fuss' about the term and I hope the book may have helped to give some answers to what this fuss has been about. I am not interested in going to the wall to defend the term 'Emerging Church' or artificially to extend its life. My concern has been to bear witness to my belief that it points to a conversation that has wrestled with issues of deep and lasting importance for ecclesiology. I believe that it has also pointed to examples of the Church's practice that are worthy of serious reflection, both because they demonstrate how traditions of belief and practice have been evolving in the recent past and because, in at least some cases, they have gifts to offer to the Church's future as it emerges under God.

Now to God be glory in the Church and in Christ Jesus, to all generations, for ever and ever, Amen.

Bibliography

Baker, J. and Gay, D., *Alternative Worship*, London: SPCK and Grand: Rapids, MI: Baker, 2004.

Barth, K., *Church Dogmatics*, Edinburgh: T & T Clark, 1939–69.

Barth, K., *The Teaching of the Church Regarding Baptism*, London: SCM Press, 1948.

Bauckham, R., *The Theology of the Book of Revelation*, Cambridge, Cambridge University Press, 1993.

Beall, P. and Keys Baker, M., *Folk Arts in Renewal*, London: Hodder & Stoughton, 1983.

Beaudoin, T., *Virtual Faith*, San Francisco: Jossey Bass, 1998.

Bevans, S., *Models of Contextual Theology*, Maryknoll: Orbis, 1992.

Bliss, K., *We The People: A Book about Laity*, London: SCM Press, 1963.

*Bolger, R. and Gibbs, E., *Emerging Churches*, Grand Rapids: Baker Academic, 2006.

Bosch, D., *Believing in the Future*, Valley Forge, PA: Trinity Press International, 1995.

Bosch, D., *Transforming Mission*, Maryknoll: Orbis, 1991.

Bradshaw, P. (ed.), *The New SCM Dictionary of Liturgy and Worship*, London: SCM Press, 2006.

Bretherton, L. & Walker, A. (eds), *Remembering Our Future: Explorations in Deep Church*, Milton Keynes: Paternoster, 2007.

Brown, C., *The Death of Christian Britain*, London: Routledge, 2001.

Burch Brown, F., *Good Taste, Bad Taste and Christian Taste*, Oxford: Oxford University Press, 2003.

Burch Brown, F., *Inclusive Yet Discerning: Navigating Worship Artfully*, Grand Rapids, MI: Eerdmans, 2009.

Carson, D., *Becoming Conversant with the Emerging Church*, Grand Rapids, MI: Zondervan, 2005.

Clements, K., Faith on the Frontier, Edinburgh: T & T Clark and Geneva: World Council of Churches, 1999.

Cone, J. H., *God of the Oppressed*, Maryknoll, NY: Orbis/London: SPCK, 1975.

Daggers, J., 'The Emergence of Feminist Theology from Christian Feminism in Britain', in Charlotte Methuen (ed.), *Time – Utopia – Eschatology*, 1999 Yearbook of the European Society of Women in Theological Research, Leuven: Peeters, 1999, pp. 137–44.

Daggers, J., 'The Rehabilitation of Eve: British "Christian Women's" Theology, 1972–1990', in Susan Frank Parsons (ed.), *Challenging Women's Orthodoxies in the Context of Faith*, Aldershot: Ashgate, 2000, pp. 53–71.

Daggers, J., '"Working for Change in the Position of Women in the Church": Christian Women's Information and Resources (CWIRES) and the British "Christian Women's" Movement, 1972–1990', *Feminist Theology* 26 (January 2001), pp. 44–69.

Davie, D., *A Gathered Church*, London: Routledge & Kegan Paul, 1978.

Donovan, V., *Christianity Rediscovered*, London: SCM Press, 1982.

Finney, P. C., *Seeing Beyond the Word: Visual Arts and the Calvinist Tradition*, Grand Rapids: Eerdmans, 1999.

Ford, D. (ed.), *The Modern Theologians*, Oxford: WileyBlackwell, 1996.

Forrester, D. (ed.), *Theology and Practice*, London: Epworth, 1990.

Forrester, D. & Gay, D. (eds), *Worship and Liturgy in Context*, London: SCM Press, 2009.

Foster, R., *Celebration of Discipline*, London: Hodder & Stoughton, 1978.

Gorringe, T., *The Education of Desire*, London: SCM Press, 2001.

Gorringe, T., *Furthering Humanity: A Theology of Culture*, Aldershot: Ashgate, 2004.

Graham, E. Walton, H. and Ward, F., *Theological Reflections: Methods*, London: SCM Press, 2005.

de Gruchy, J. W., *Christianity, Art and Transformation*, Cambridge: Cambridge University Press, 2001.

Hart, T., *Faith Thinking*, London: SPCK, 1995.

Hauerwas, S., *The Peaceable Kingdom: A Primer in Christian Ethics*, London: SCM Press, 2003.

Hauerwas, S., *Performing The Faith*, London: SPCK/Grand Rapids, MI: Baker Academic/Brazos, 2004.

Hauerwas, S., *With The Grain of the Universe*, Grand Rapids, MI: Brazos/London: SCM Press, 2001.

Howard, R., *The Rise and Fall of the Nine O'Clock Service: A Cult Within the Church*, London: Mowbray/Continuum, 1996.

Howard, T., *Evangelical Is Not Enough*, Nashville: Thomas Nelson, 1984.

Hughes, R., *The Shock of the New*, London: Thames and Hudson, 1991.

Husbands, M. & Greenman, J. P. (eds), *Ancient Faith for the Church's Future*, Downers Grove, IL: InterVarsity Press, 2008.

Hutter, R., *Bound to be Free: Evangelical Catholic Engagements in Ecclesiology, Ethics and Ecumenism*, Grand Rapids, MI: Eerdmans, 2004.

Jasper, R. (ed.), *The Renewal of Worship*, Oxford: Oxford University Press, 1965.

Jencks, Charles, *The Language of Post-Modern Architecture*, Rizzoli, NY: Wiley, 1977.

Kraemer, H., *A Theology of the Laity*, London: Lutterworth, 1958.

Leech, K., *The Social Gospel*, London: Sheldon, 1981.

McGrath, A. E., *Christian Theology: An Introduction*, Oxford: Blackwell, 1994.

McGrath, A. E., *The Future of Christianity*, Oxford: Blackwell, 2002.

MacIntyre, A., *After Virtue*, London: Duckworth, 1987 (1981).

Mannion, G. and Mudge, L. S. (eds.), *The Routledge Companion to the Christian Church*, New York/Abingdon: Routledge, 2008.

Mast, G., *In Remembrance and Hope: The Ministry and Vision of Howard G. Hageman*, Grand Rapids, MI: Eerdmans, 1998.

Metz, J. B., *The Emergent Church*, London: SCM Press, 1980.

Milbank, J., *Theology and Social Theory*, Oxford: Blackwell, 1990.

Milbank, J. and Oliver, S. (eds), *The Radical Orthodoxy Reader*, London: Routledge, 2009.

Moltmann, J., *The Church in the Power of the Spirit*, London: SCM Press, 1992 (1977).

Moore, M. E., 'Editorial', *International Journal of Practical Theology* 10:2 (2006), pp. 163–7.

Morley, J., *All Desires Known*, London: SPCK, 1992 (1988).

Morton, R., *Household of Faith*, Glasgow: Iona Community, 1951.

Neill, S. and Weber, H.-R., *The Layman in Christian History*, London: SCM Press/Geneva: World Council of Churches, 1963.

*Nelstrop, L. and Percy, M. (eds), *Evaluating Fresh Expressions*, Norwich: Canterbury Press, 2008.

Newbigin, L., *The Gospel in a Pluralist Society*, London: SPCK, 1989.

BIBLIOGRAPHY

Newbigin, L., *The Open Secret*, Grand Rapids, MI: Eerdmans, 1978.
Newbigin, L., *The Other Side of 1984*, Geneva: Risk/World Council of Churches, 1983.
Newbigin, L., *Unfinished Agenda*, Edinburgh: St Andrew Press, 1993.

Ong, W., *Orality and Literacy*, London: Routledge, 1982.

Percy, M. and Nelstrop, L. (eds), *Evaluating Fresh Expressions*, Norwich: Canterbury Press, 2008.
Puglisi, J. F. (ed.), *Liturgical Renewal as a Way to Christian Unity*, Collegeville, MN: Pueblo/Liturgical Press, 2005.

Ricoeur, P., *Freud and Philosophy: An Essay on Interpretation*, New Haven, CT: Yale University Press, 1970.
Riddell, M. Pierson, M. and Kirkpatrick, C., *The Prodigal Project*, London: SPCK, 2000.
Roberts, P., *Alternative Worship in the Church of England*, Nottingham: Grove Books, 1999.

Saayman, W. and Kritzinger, K. (eds), *Mission in Bold Humility: David Bosch's Work Considered*, Maryknoll, NY: Orbis, 1997.
Sanneh, L., *Translating the Message*, Maryknoll, NY: Orbis, 1989.
Schreiter, R., *Constructing Local Theologies*, Maryknoll, NY: Orbis, 1985.
Sheppard, D., *Bias to the Poor*, London: Hodder, 1983.
Shirky, C., *Here Comes Everybody*, London: Penguin, 2008.
Sider, R., *Rich Christians in an Age of Hunger*, Nashville: Thomas Nelson, 1977.
Smith, J. K. A., 'Emerging Church: A Guide for the Perplexed', *Reformed Worship* 77 (2005).
Smith, J. K. A., *Radical Orthodoxy: A New Tradition*, London: Routledge, 1999.
Smith, J. K. A., *Who's Afraid of Postmodernism?*, Grand Rapids, MI: Baker Academic, 2006.
St Hilda Community, *Women Included*, London: SPCK, 1991.

Taylor, C., *A Secular Age*, Cambridge, MA: Belknap/Harvard University Press, 2005.
Thistleton, A., *New Horizons in Hermeneutics*, London: Harper Collins, 1992.
Todd, M., *The Culture of Protestantism in Early Modern Scotland*, New Haven, CT: Yale University Press, 2002.

Vanhoozer, K., Anderson, C. A. and Sleasman, M. J. (eds), *Everyday Theology*, Grand Rapids, MI: Baker Academic, 2007.

Vischer, L., *Christian Worship in Reformed Churches Past and Present*, Grand Rapids, MI: Eerdmans, 2003.

Visser t'Hooft, W. A. and Oldham, J. H., *The Church and its Function in Society*, London: Allen & Unwin, 1937.

Volf, M., *After Our Likeness*, Grand Rapids, MI: Eerdmans, 1998.

Wainwright, G., *Doxology*, New York: Oxford University Press, 1980.

Wainwright, G., *Worship With One Accord: Where Liturgy and Ecumenism Embrace*, New York: Oxford University Press, 1997.

Wallis, J., *Agenda for Biblical People*, New York; Harper Collins, 1976.

Walls, A. and Ross, C., *Mission in the Twentieth Century*, London: Darton, Longman and Todd, 2008.

Ward, P., *Growing Up Evangelical*, London: SPCK, 1996.

Ward, P., *Participation and Mediation: A Practical Theology for the Liquid Church*, London: SCM Press, 2008.

Ward, P., *Selling Worship*, Milton Keynes: Paternoster, 2005.

Watson, N., *Introducing Feminist Ecclesiology*, London: Continuum, 2002.

Webber, R., *Ancient-Future Evangelism: Making Your Church a Faith-forming Community*, Grand Rapids, MI: Baker Academic, 2003.

Webber, R., *Ancient-Future Faith: Rethinking Evangelicalism for a Post-Modern World*, Grand Rapids, MI: Baker Academic, 1999.

Webber, R., 'Call to an Ancient Evangelical Future', published by Robert Webber and Phil Kenyon, www.aefcenter.org/read.html, (accessed 17 March 2009).

Webber, R., *Common Roots: Call to Evangelical Maturity*, Grand Rapids, MI: Zondervan, 1978.

Webber, R., *Evangelicals on the Canterbury Trail: Why Evangelicals are Attracted to the Liturgical Church*, New York: Continuum, 1985.

Williams, D. H., *Evangelicals and Tradition: The Formative Influence of the Early Church*, Grand Rapids, MI: Baker Academic, 2005.

Williams, R., *The Wound of Knowledge*, London: Darton, Longman and Todd, 1990.

Wilson-Dickson, A., *The Story of Christian Music*, Oxford: Lion, 1992.

Wink, W., *Naming the Powers*, Philadelphia: Fortress, 1984.

Wink, W., *Engaging the Powers*, Philadelphia: Fortress, 1986.

Wink, W., *Unmasking the Powers*, Philadelphia: Fortress, 1992.

Wolterstorff, N., *Art In Action: Toward a Christian Aesthetic*, Grand Rapids, MI: Eerdmans, 1980.

Yates, T., *Christian Mission in the Twentieth Century*, Cambridge: Cambridge University Press, 1996.

Yoder, J. H., *Body Politics: Five Practices of the Christian Community before the Watching World*, Scottsdale, PA: Herald Press, 2001.

Yoder, J. H., *The Politics of Jesus*, second edition, Grand Rapids, MI: Eerdmans, 1992.

Other works

Mission Shaped Church, London: Church House Publishing, 2004.

Religious Trends, Swindon: Christian Research, 2001–8.

Index of Names

Adam, David 44

Baker, Jonny xv n10, 7,
    65n35, 98
Barth, Karl 3, 4, 15, 27, 29,
    34, 45, 50, 61, 66, 103,
    107, 118
Bauckham, Richard 119, 120
Beall, Patricia 14n36
Bebbington, David 97n10
Bell, John 10
Beaudoin, Tom 88
Beauduin, Lambert 32
Berrigan, Daniel 44
Bevans, Stephen 16n41, 83
Bolger, Ryan xv n10, 6, 28,
    76, 87
Bosch, David 16n41, 65n37,
    82
Bretherton, Luke 29n23
Brown, Stewart J 33n30
Brueggemann, Walter 81, 103
Burch Brown, Frank 12n30
Byassee, Jason 42

Calvin, John 11
Caputo, John D. 103

Carlyle, Thomas 25n10
Carson, Donald xi n1
Case-Winters, Anna 2
Casel, Odo 32
Chalke, Steve 104
Clements, K. 34n33
Coakley, Sarah 104
Cone, James 80
Costas, Orlando 79
Cullman, Oscar 80

Daggers, Jenny 14n37
Darby, John Nelson 25n10
Davie, Donald 11
Day, Dorothy 44, 79
de Gruchy, John W. 11n27
de Waal, Esther 44
Donovan, Vincent 83

Eliot, T.S. 13

Fergusson, David 11n27,
    12n30, 104
Finney, Paul Corby 11n27
Ford, David 104
Forrester, Duncan 5n15, 68
Foster, Richard 38, 43